THE PEOPLE OF ASSAM

Origin and Composition

THE PEOPLES OF ASSAM

Dr. B. M. Das

The Peoples of Assam

ISBN: 978-81-212-0093-6

Reprinted in 2010 in India by
Gyan Publishing House,
23, Main Ansari Road Darya Ganj
New Delhi-110002
Phones : 23282060, 23261060
Fax : (011) 23285914
E-mail: gyanbooks@vsnl.com
Website : http : // www.gyanbooks.com

Printed at : Gian Ridhi Offset Printers, Delhi

*Dedicated to the sacred memory of
Late Professor Lalita Prasad Vidyarthi, eminent
anthropologist of our time, whose friendship was
a constant source of intellectual stimulation to me*

Dedicated to th[illegible] [illegible] memory of

Late Professor Lalita [illegible] Vidya[illegible]

[illegible]thropologist [illegible] whose [illegible] was

[illegible]

Contents

PREFACE TO THE SECOND EDITION

Since the publication of the book in 1987, some new data relating, more particularly, to the relative positions of the various population groups of Assam have been made available by different scholars through their studies. These finding have been included in the present edition. Hence, it is an enlarged and revised version of the first edition. A subtitile called, "Origin and Composition" has also been added.

This edition has been prepared at the request of Sri Amit Garg, Gyan Publishing House, Delhi. I am thankful to him for bringing out this edition.

New Delhi, February, 2003 **B.M. Das**

PREFACE TO THE FIRST EDITION

I have written many articles in Assamese as well as in English in various magazines and journals in India and abroad, and also have delivered lectures in different parts of the country and abroad on the ethnic composition of the people of Northeast India. My friend Professor L.P. Vidyarthi during our last meeting in Guwahati in 1985 suggested me to compile the relevant material and arrange the same in the form of a book in popular or non-technical manner so as to reach general readers and at the same time prove useful to students of anthropology. Unfortunately, Professor Vidyarthi has left us for his heavenly abode, but his suggestion had a telling effect all the time in my mind and finally, I decided to put the material in a book form.

The present book is thus based on my earlier work. Moreover, it contains some of the selected material from earlier writings by me as well as with my colleagues. However, many new information have been incorporated in proper contexts and the matter has been presented entirely with a new approach.

I am grateful to my good friend and colleague Professor A.C. Bhagabati for his kindly examining the typescript thoroughly and critically, and for offering valuable suggestions for improvement. I am thankful to my colleagues Professor Priya Bala Das and Dr. Renuka Das for their kindly going through the typescript. My thanks are due to those scholars whose works I have used or referred to.

I thank Sri Rati Kanta Das, who did the typing, and also to those who directly or indirectly helped me in bringing out this publication. I am thankful to Mr. B.P. Garg Managing Director, Gyan Publishing House, Delhi for taking the responsibility for publishing the book.

My endeavour will be rewarded if the book proves to be useful to the readers.

Guwahati, January 4, 1987 **B.M. DAS**

Chapter 1
Introduction

Assam, more particularly the Brahmaputra Valley, is a meeting place of two major races of mankind, namely, the Caucasoid and the Mongoloid. As a matter of fact, this valley served the purpose of a road linking India with Southeast Asia, and therefore, the people of Assam have a some sort of relationship with the people of Southeast Asia. Various population groups of different ethnic affiliations used this route at different intervals of time since time immemorial laying the racial and cultural foundation of the people of this region. This route may be reached from the western direction through the valleys formed by the Brahmaputra and the Ganges. The Caucasic people entered Assam from western direction following this route, while the Mongoloid people came to Assam from the North and the East. On the northern side, there are several passes through Tibet, Bhutan and Nepal, which were used by these Mongoloid people. On the eastern direction there lie two major routes, one, the Assam-Myanmar route via Nagaland, Manipur and Mizoram connecting this region with Southeast Asia, and the other, through Patkai ranges in the northeast corner. This region was approachable by sea route also, that is, by the Bay of Bengal.

During the British regime Assam covered a much larger geographical area. The present day Meghalaya, Nagaland, Mizoram, parts of Arunachal Pradesh were within Assam. Besides, a small portion of Bangladesh was also included in Assam. Hence, at one time, by Assam it meant the whole of this region. After partition of India, that part of Assam, namely, Sylhet was transferred to East Pakistan (now Bangladesh). In 1963 Nagaland, which formed a district of Assam, was carved out to give birth to a separate state. Then, the new state of Meghalaya covering the districts of Khasi and Jaintia hills and the Garo hills of Assam came into being in 1971. In the same year the Lushai hills district of Assam was separated from Assam to form Mizoram. Again, in 1972 the former North East Frontier Agency (NEFA) was given the status of a Union Territory by a new name Arunachal Pradesh, which became a state. Thus, in course of time Assam was divided to give birth to several new states and thereby, Assam was made smaller and smaller in size. At present there are seven states in Northeast India. These are Arunachal, Assam, Meghalaya, Mizoram,

Manipur, Nagaland and Tripura (Fig. 1). Manipur and Tripura were two princely states during the British rule. Northeast India comprising these seven states lying between the latitudes of 22° and 29° N and the longitudes of 89° 46' and 97°5' E, may be regarded as one geoethnic unit taking into account certain factors like geographical location, cultural heritage, historical background and ethnic composition. To this may be added Sikkim and the northern districts of West Bengal, which however, will not be taken into account in the present study, though Sikkim is a member state of North East Council. Under these circumstances, the people of Assam, their culture, more particularly the racial elements in them, could not be properly studied without taking into consideration the neighbouring regions of Northeast India (Table 1), and hence, occasionally reference to some populations of this region will have to be made.

Arunachal Pradesh : Arunachal Pradesh is the largest state of Northeast India, covering an area of about 83,600 sq. km. The state is hilly. The state is thinly populated (10 per sq. km.), the total of population being about 8.6 lakhs, of which about 5.5 lakhs are tribal (63.66%). A large number of tribes live in Arunachal. Some of the major tribes are the Adi (Abor) of Siang district; the Nishi (Dafla), Apatani, Galong, Tagin of Subansiri district, the Khamti, Singpho and

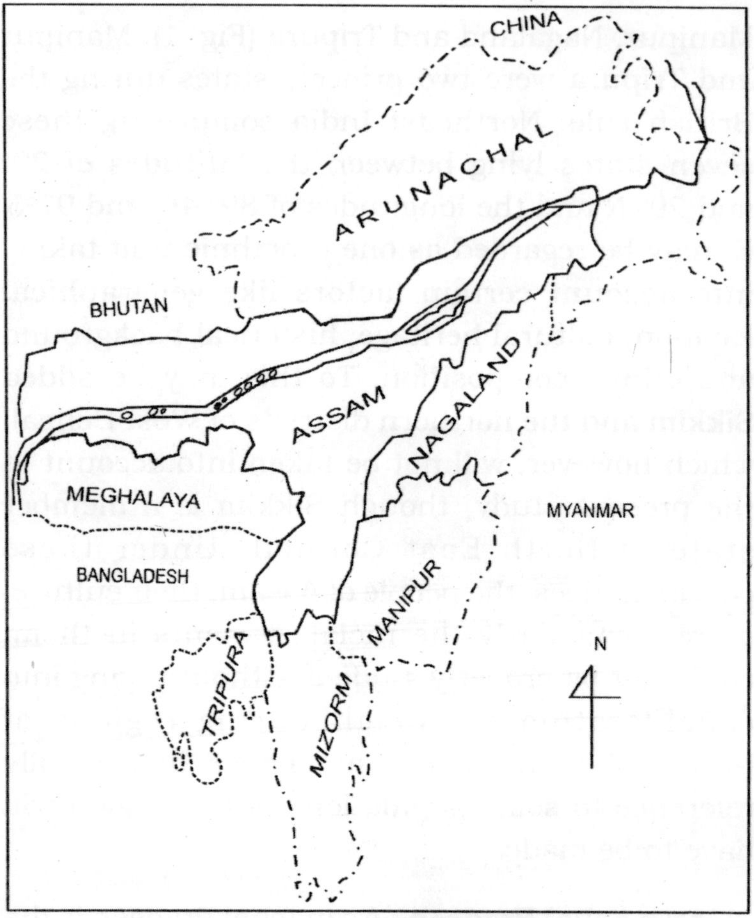

Fig. 1. Map of Northeast India.

Mishimi of Lohit district; the Monpa, Aka and Sherdukpan of Kameng district and the Wanchoo, Nocte and Tangsa of Tirap district.

Manipur : 34.41 per cent (about 6.3 lakhs) of the population of Manipur is tribal, the total population being about 18.4 lakhs and the density being 82 per sq. km. The state covers an area of about 22,360 sq. km. The tribal people mostly live in the hills surrounding the Imphal valley. The tribal population is mostly formed by various Naga tribes, Kuki tribes and Mizo (Lushai) tribes. The valley is dominated by the Meithes, who belong to Other Backward Classes. A section of the population is formed by the Manipuri Muslims.

Meghalaya : The hill state of Meghalaya is predominantly a tribal state. 85.53 per cent (about 15 lakhs) of the total population of about 17.7 lakhs is tribal. The area of the state is about 22,500 sq. km., almost equal to that of Manipur. But the density (79 per sq. km.) is slightly lower than that in Manipur. The two major tribes are the Garo (population more than 3.6 lakhs) distributed in the western part of the state and the Khasi-Jaintia group (population about 5 lakhs) occupying the eastern region. Members of some tribes, like the Dimasa, Hajong, Hmar, Kuki, Lushai, Man (Tai speaking), Karbi, Naga, Boro Kachari, Rabha in small numbers are also met with in Meghalaya.

Mizoram : Mizoram is also a hill state covering an area of about 21,000 sq. km., with a population of about 7 lakhs, the density being 33 per sq. km, much less than that in Meghalaya and Nagaland. Most of the people (94.75%) of Mizoram are tribals. The two numerically dominant tribes of the state are the Mizo (Lushai) and the Kuki, each of which includes several subgroups. In addition to these two major tribes, representatives of about ten tribes including the Dimasa, Chakma, Garo, Haiong, Hmar, Karbi and Khasi also live in Mizoram.

Nagaland : Another hill state of this region is Nagaland. It, covering an area of about 16,500 sq. km, is smaller in size than Mizoram and Meghalaya. The state provides shelter to about 12 lakh people, the density being 73 per sq. km. The percentage of tribal population of the state is 87.70. Nagaland is the homeland of the Nagas, which is some sort of a generic name for the various Naga tribes like the Angami, Ao, Chang, Konyak, Lhota, Phom, Rengma, Sema. Besides the Nagas, some other tribes, for example, the Garo, Kuki, Kachari, Karbi, etc. are also found in Nagaland though their numbers are much smaller than that of the Naga tribe as a whole.

Tripura : Tripura covering about 10,500 sq. km. is the smallest state of all the states of Northeast India, with a population of about 27.5 lakhs. Hence, the density is 263 per sq. km. About 31 per cent of the people are tribals. The most numerically dominant original tribal group is formed by the Tripuri (Tippera). Some of the other tribes of Tripura are the Chakma, Mag, Riang, Uchai, Garo, Khasi, Lushai, Kuki, etc. There are several OBC communities also in Tripura.

Table 1 : Population Figures of Northeast India

State	Area in sq. km.	Total Popul -ation	Tribal Popul- -ation	Density (Popula- -tion per sq. km.)	Sex Ratio (Female per 1000 Males)	Percentage of Tribal Population
Assam	78523	22414322	2874441	286	923	12.83
Arunachal Pradesh	83578	864558	550351	10	859	63.66
Meghalaya	22489	1774778	1517927	79	955	85.53
Nagaland	16572	1209546	1060822	73	886	87.70
Mizoram	21087	689756	653565	33	921	94.75
Manipur	22356	1837149	632173	82	953	34.41
Tripura	10477	2757205	853345	263	945	30.95

Source: Census of India 1991, final Population totals, RGI.

The Prehistoric Time

It is true that a comprehensive picture of the life and culture of the prehistoric time of Northeast India is yet to emerge fully, but there is no denial of the fact that this part of the country has a rich prehistoric cultural heritage, as is evidenced by the discovery of a good number of prehistoric sites from different parts of the region. The fact was brought to light by the British scholars and administrators more than hundred years ago. The first report on the stone age of Assam was published as early as in 1867. Since then through the efforts of several British scholars new information were reported. This was intensified and systematic researches were undertaken by

Indian scholars including local experts after Independence. As a result at present several laudable works are available at hand. The relics of prehistoric cultures have been collected from different sites in Assam, Meghalaya, Arunachal Pradesh and Manipur on the basis of which a general outline of the prehistoric past of Northeast India can be reconstructed.

The Garo Hills of Meghalaya, Lohit district of Arunachal Pradesh and Tengnopal district of Manipur have yielded several stone artifacts representing Palaeolithic culture. Unfortunately, no remains of Palaeolithic culture have yet been reported from Assam, Mizoram, Tripura and Nagaland. On the basis of typology of relics of the Garo Hills three cultural phases of Palaeolithic period have been identified (Sankalia and Sharma 1984). These are: Lower Palaeolithic characterized by pebbletools, handaxes, cleavers and choppers; Middle Palaeolithic characterized by flake-tool industry; and Upper Palaeolithic characterized by blade-tool industry.

Stone tools (microliths) representing the Eastern Mesolithic culture (commonly known as Hoabinhian culture) have also been collected from certain areas in Meghalaya, Arunachal and Nagaland, which suggest existence of Mesolithic culture in Northeast India.

The Neolithic culture was fairly widespread all

over Northeast India, except Mizoram and Tripura which are yet to provide more evidence. The Neolithic tool tradition of Northeast India is characterized by shouldered celts, quadriangular axes and adzes, cord-marked pottery, etc. Sharma (1984) believes that the Neolithic cultures of Northeast India have affinities with the Eastern Asiatic Neolithic tradition, which extended as far west as the foot-hills of the Vindyas and Middle Gangetic valley. Thus, the Neolithic culture appears to have spread from Eastern Asia to Eastern India through Northeast India. The period of diffusion may be between 6000 and 5000 B.C. as per dated materials of Eastern India.

In this connection it may perhaps be mentioned that certain prehistoric cultural traditions or traits still persist among some people of Northeast India suggesting continuation of cultural traits though in changed form from prehistoric time to modern time. Digging stick, hoe, hand made pottery may be cited as examples.

Ancient Assam

In ancient times, Assam constituted a part of the country known as Pragjyotisha (and/or Kamarupa). Mention of Pragjyotishpur is found in the great epics, the *Mahabharata* and the *Ramayana* and also in some of the Puranas indicating antiquity of the country. During the time of these two epics, Pragjyotisha was a much larger country. In the *Mahabharata,* it is mentioned that the boundary of Pragjyotisha extended up to the Bay of Bengal in the south and Karatowa River in the west. From the Sabha Parva of the *Mahabharata* it is learnt that the army of Bhagadatta, the king of Pragjyotisha, consisted of Kiratas, Chinas and many other warriors dwelling in the coast of the sea, suggesting the fact that the territory of Bhagadatta reached the sea-shore. The *Ramayana* tells that the western boundary was formed by the river Koshi in Purnia district of modern Bihar. Some parts of Nepal and Bhutan were also included within the territory of ancient Pragjyotisha.

The *Bhagabata Purana* while dealing with the story of Narakasura refers to Pragjyotish. Mention of Pragjyotish is also found in the *Markendeya Purana.* Naraka had its capital in Pragjyotishpura, about which in the *Kalika Purana* written in the tenth century A.D., it is stated that "Formerly Brahma staying here created the stars: so the city is called Pragjyotishpura, a city equal to the city of Indra" (c.f. Barua 1951 : 11). Gait (1963 :15) writes, "Prag means former or eastern, and jyotisha, a star, astrology, shinning. Pragjyotishpura may, therefore, be taken to mean the city of Eastern Astrology. The name is interesting in connection with the reputation which the country has always held as a land of magic and incantation and with the view that it was in Assam that the Tantric form of Hinduism originated". But scholars like B.K. Kakati (c.f. Barua 1951) are inclined to say that the term has originated from the topographical features of the land. In Austric language Pagar-juh (jo)-tic (c=ch) means a region of extensive high hills and which Pragjyotish is. Pragjyotish may be a Sanskritized version of the original non-Aryan term.

In the mediaeval times, Pragjyotisha came to be known as Kamarupa. In the *Kalika Purana*, written in the tenth century A.D., it has been stated that soon after Naraka of Mithila ascended the throne, the name Pragjyotisha was changed to Kamarupa.

Mythology tells us about the origin of the name Kamarupa. After the death of Sati at her father Dakshya's place, when Siva was doing penance, the other Gods became afraid and requested Kamadeva to make Siva fall in love and thereby break his penance. Kamadeva did that. But Siva was so angry with Kamadeva that by a fiercy glance of his third eye he burnt Kamadeva into ashes. At the request of Rati, the wife of Kamadeva he was granted recovery of his original form. Thus, the country where Kamadeva regained his form is called Kamarupa.

Rajshekhar, a poet of the royal court of Mahipal, the king of Kannauja while describing Aryavarta referred to Pragjyotisha, and not to

Kamarupa. On the other hand Alberuni, who during the eleventh century A.D., accompanied Sultan Mahmud to India mentioned the name of Kamarupa while dealing with eastern India. Again, Hiuen Tsiang, a Chinese pilgrim who came to Kamarupa during the reign of Bhaskaravarman in the seventh century A.D., mentioned that to enter Kamarupa (Kia-no-leu-po) he had to cross a large river called the Karatowa. He gave a very good account of Kamarupa. Thus, perhaps it can be said that till the twelfth century A.D., both the names, Kamarupa and Pragjyotisha were used indiscriminately to refer to almost the same country. But it must be kept in mind that the political boundary of ancient Pragjyotisha as well as Kamarupa was changed during different periods.

The modern name Assam is of comparatively recent origin. Opinions differ as regards how the name Assam was derived. A group of Shan invaders entered the Brahmaputra Valley in the beginning of the thirteenth century. The local people referred to them as the 'Asama' which means 'unequalled' or 'peerless'. In course of time they came to be known as the Ahoms, the modern name of these Shan people and the country was called Asama after the name of the people. Another opinion is that in 'Tai' language 'cham' means 'to be defeated'. With the addition of an Assamese prefix 'a', it became Acham, which means 'undefeated', 'conquerors'. Asama, peerless, may be a Sanskritisation of the earlier form Acham. Again, following another authority the term Asama may be derived from Ha-cham, which in Boro language means the low or level country. Thus, in this case the name of the people is after the county where they lived. The modern name Assam is an Anglicised form of the Assamese name Asom.

The early inhabitants of Northeast India were also known to the Hindu world of North India. It has already been stated that the hilly regions as well as some parts of the plains of Northeast India is the homeland of several Indo-Mongoloid tribes. In ancient literature the Indo-Mongoloids are referred to as the Kiratas. Mention of the Kiratas is noted in the Vedic literature. The *Mahabharata* tells that the Himalayan region, particularly the Eastern Himalayas were the abode of the Kiratas. Bhima in his eastward soujarn encountered seven Kirata rulers. Bhagadatta joined in Kurukshetra battle with his soldiers, most of whom were Kiratas. The Kiratas have found place in the *Ramayana* as well. These are, however, some of the examples.

Lord Krishna occupies a unique place in the Mythology of Northeast India. In the Puranas and Tantras Naraka finds place very often. Naraka was born of the earth by Vishnu in his pig incarnation. He was brought up by Janak, king of Videha (North Bihar). He married Maya, the daughter of the king of Vidarbha. Naraka had his capital in Pragjyotishpur (modern Guwahati). He provided settlements to a large number of Brahmans in his kingdom. At first he was very much favoured by Vishnu. But he became so tyrannical, vain and over ambitious that he lost Vishnu's favour. Eventually, Vishnu in his incarnation of Krishna slained Naraka. In North Guwahati there is a temple called Asvakranta, which literally means 'ascended by horse'. It is said that when Krishna came to invade Praghyotish, he halted there. His horses left foot prints in the form of small holes.

Ban, King of Sonitpur (modern Tezpur) was contemporary of Naraka. He had one daughter, Usha by name. Aniruddha, grandson of Krishna being attracted by her beauty came to Sonitpur and secretly married her according to Gandharbha custom. He was captured by Ban. Krishna came all the way from Dwaraka to rescue Aniruddha. A fierce battle was fought between Krishna and Ban. Ban was defeated. This battle is very often referred to as Hari (Krishna)-Hara (Siva) Yodha (battle). Because Siva took side of Ban, a stern devotee of the former. It is regarded as a conflict between Vaishnavism (which came to east at a later date) and Saivism (which was there from earlier time). Even now ruins of the kingdom of Ban are seen in Tezpur.

There was a king Bhismaka by name. His

capital was Kundila, situated near modern Sadiya. The remains of the capital are still there. Bhismaka had a very beautiful daughter called Rukmini. Krishna was attracted by her beauty. Rukmini too wanted to have Krishna as her husband. But Bhismaka arranged to give her to Sishupal. Rukmini sent a secret message to Krishna, who came to Kundila on the day fixed for the marriage and suddenly carried her off. Bhismaknagar, the fortress of king Bhismaka is located in the present day Dibang valley of Arunachal Pradesh. Krishna and Rukmini on their way back to Dwaraka were entertained by Siva and his consort Parvati at a place called Malinithan in West Siang district of Arunachal Pradesh.

Parasurama carrying the order of his father Jamadagni killed his mother Renuka. To get rid of his sin he visited the holy places throughout the country and ultimately came to Brahmakunda in the present Lohit district of Arunachal. He cut a passage from the Kunda for water to come out by digging the bank. After that he took bath there, when the axe which got stuck to his hand as a result of the crime committed, dropped. The spot where it fell down came to be known as Parasuramkunda. Now this is a holy kunda visited by people from all parts of the region. Brahmakunda has also a legend behind it involving Brahma and Rishi Santanu and his wife Amogha. In the *Kalika Purana* these stories have been narrated.

Arjuna during his 'agyat bash' came to Manipur and married Chitrangada, the princes. Bhima took Hidimba of Hidimbapur as his wife. It is believed that the first line of Kachari king started from Ghototkach, the son of Bhima and Hidimba. When Ghototkach was killed in the battle of Kurukshetra, his son Sasempha ascended the throne. Vasistha did his 'toposya' near Guwahati. Several such legends are prevalent in the Mythology of this region.

Assam : Its People

Assam covers an area of about 78,500 sq. km. It is inhabited by about 22,41,400 individuals of which about 28.75 lakhs are tribals, the percentage being 12.83. The population density is 286 per sq. km, being the highest of all the states in Northeast India.

Assam can be divided into three geographic areas, the Brahmaputra Valley, the Barak valley and the hilly area formed by Karbi Anglong and North Cachar Hills districts, which separates the two valleys. The Brahmaputra valley again be divided into three zones, namely, Upper, Middle and Lower. The Assamese people mostly live in this valley.

Population Groups

The people of Assam can be divided into different categories on the basis of different criteria like race, language, religion. As has already been mentioned, Assam is the homeland of various populations belonging to two major races, namely, the Mongoloid and the Caucasoid. All the tribes of Assam are of Mongoloid origin. In addition to the tribes some other Mongoloid populations are met with in this region which are not recognised as tribes. The other non-tribal section of the people of Assam is affiliated to the Caucasoid race.

The language of the Assamese people, known as the Assamese, belongs to the Indo-Aryan linguistic family. The Mongoloid population can be divided into certain groups on the basis of the languages spoken by them or were spoken by their ancestors when they came to Assam, but in course of time abandoned their languages in favour of the Assamese language. These linguistic groups are: Tibeto-Burman, Tai and Austroasiatic.

The majority of the people are Hindu by religion. A sizable section is formed by the Muslims. Christian, Sikh, Jain and Buddhist people are also there, but in very small numbers. Some practise tribal religions.

Looking at from another angle, the people of Assam can be divided into two broad categories : tribal and non-tribal. Government has given a list of scheduled tribes. [The Scheduled Castes and

Scheduled Tribes Orders (Amendment) Act, 1976 (No. 108 of 1976, dated the 18th September, 1976)]: Census of India 1981:

List of Assam Tribes

(I) In the autonomous district :

1. Chakma
2. Dimasa, Kachari
3. Garo
4. Hajong
5. Hmar
6. Khasi, Jaintia, Synteng, Pnar, War, Bhoi, Lyngngam
7. Any Kuki Tribes
8. Lakher
9. Man (Tai speaking)
10. Any Mizo (Lushai) Tribes
11. Mikir
12. Any Naga Tribes
13. Pawi
14. Synteng

(As a matter of fact, the terms Jaintia, Synteng and Pnar denote the same population.)

(II) In the State of Assam excluding the autonomous districts:

1. Barmans in Cachar
2. Boro, Borokachari

3. Deori
4. Hojai
5. Kachari, Sonwal
6. Lalung
7. Mech
8. Miri
9. Rabha

The non-tribal category includes three major groups, namely, the 'Caste-Hindu' or General Caste, the Scheduled Castes and the Other Backward Classes (OBC).

Government has identified the following populations as the Scheduled Castes.

List of Scheduled Castes

1. Bansphor
2. Bhuinmali, Mali
3. Brittial Bania, Bania
4. Dhupi, Dhobi
5. Dugla, Dholi
6. Hira
7. Jalkeot
8. Jhalo, Malo, Jhalo-Malo
9. Kaibartta, Jaliya
10. Lalbegi
11. Mahara
12. Mehtar, Bhangi

13. Muchi, Rishi
14. Namasudra
15. Patni
16. Sutradhar

The Central list of the Other Backward Classes include the following communities:

1. Ahom
2. Baria
3. Barjubi
4. Baroi
5. Barui
6. Choudang
7. Chutia, Chutiya
8. Ganak in Districts of Cachar, Karimganj and Hailakandi
9. Ghosh, Gop, Gowala, Gawala, Goal, Goala
10. Kumar, Rudra Paul of district of Cacha, Karimganj and Hailakandi
11. Kupadhar, Kushiari, Parh
12. Mahisya Das, Mahisya
13. Maimal (Muslim Fisherman)
14. Manipuri, including Manipuri Brahmin and Manipuri Muslim
15. Maria
16. Moran, Mathak

17. Mukhi
18. Napit
19. Nepali (i.e., Thapa, Gurung, Lama, Gaine, Rai, Chetri, Chatri, Chhetri, Lihu, Magar, Lohar, Dami, Sarki, i.e., (Cobbler)
20. Rajbanshi Koch
21. Sudra Das, Dey
22. Saloi
23. Sut, Soot
24. Scheduled Caste persons converted to Christianity
25. Tantripal, Tanti, Tantri
26. Tea Garden Labourers, Tea Garden Tribes, Ex-Tea Garden Labourers and Ex-Tea Garden Tribes as listed below: (not give here)
27. Teli
28. Yogi, Jogi, Jugi, Nath

Of the Tribes of Assam, the Kacharis are distributed almost all over the state. They have several sub-divisions. One is the Dimasa, who are a hill people, and are concentrated in North Cachar Hills. The Sonowal, Thengal and Jharua are met with in Upper Assam. The Kacharis of Lower and Middle Assam are very often referred to as the Boro Kachari or Boro.

The Rabhas are mostly met with in Lower Assam. They too have several sub-divisions, the main three being the Pati, Rangdani and the Maitori. The Mishings (Miri) and the Deoris inhabit some parts of Upper Assam. The Tiwas (Lalung) are mostly confined to Middle Assam, where the Hojais also live. The Meches mostly live in Lower Assam.

Some Garo settlements are found in Assam, though the Garo homeland is the Garo Hills of Meghalaya. The same is true of the Khasi and the allied populations. Nagaland is the state of the Nagas, but some of them are met with, in Assam also. The Man settlements are mostly found in the Garo Hills. The Kuki tribes and the Hmars live in the southern hilly regions of the state. The Karbis are mostly concentrated in Karbi Anglong, though many of them are scattered in some parts of the plain region, particularly in Middle and Lower Assam.

Besides the Assam tribes, which are of Mongoloid origin, some other Mongoloid populations, not included under scheduled tribes, also live in different parts of Assam in large numbers, for example, the Ahoms, Chutiyas, Morans, and the small Buddhist populations like the Tai Phake, Aiton, Turung, Duania. The Koches are also considered to be of Mongoloid origin. Many of these are included under 'Other Backward

Classes'.

The caste system is one of the most important features of the Hindu society. The names and numbers of castes, the nature and extent of caste stratification, both horizontal and vertical, caste rules and regulations, functions etc., vary from region to region in India. Unlike some other parts of India casteism is not practised very rigidly in Assamese Hindu society. Various reasons can be attributed for this liberal ethos of the Assamese society. One may be the Vaishnavite movement launched by Srimanta Sankardeva, a socio-cultural reformer and religious preacher of the fifteenth century. Another may be the fact that Assam came under the influence of the Aryan culture at a much later date and hence casteism could not gain strong foothold.

Moreover, the socio-cultural background of the earlier non-Aryan settlers of Assam might have been another factor to stand against easy spread of casteism.

In Assam in general practice, two broad categories of Hindu castes are recognized. These are the 'Bamun' (Brahmin) and the 'Sudir' (Sudra : non-Brahmin). The Sudir group includes several castes of different hierarchical positions.

In the Assamese society the Brahmins occupy the topmost position in the caste hierarchy. Their traditional occupation, is priesthood. But at present they have taken other occupation also for their livelihood.

The Brahmins are considered to be one of the oldest of the Hindu settlers in Assam. During the Chutiya dynasties some Brahmin families came to the northeastern corner of the Brahmaputra valley. That happened before the coming of the Ahoms. During the 13th or 14th century several waves of migration brought some Brahmin families to this region from Mithila or Bihar at the initiative of the local kings. Another migration took place in the 16th century. After that they were coming to Assam at different times.

The Kalitas form the most populous caste of Assam. Perhaps it may be said that the Kalita caste is a speciality of Assamese caste system. Opinions differ as regards their origin, migration and occupation. One account suggests that, they were originally Kayasthas, but as they took to agriculture they assumed a new name and formed a separate caste. According to another account they are the descendants of the Kshatriyas who fled from the wrath of Parasurama and to conceal their caste identity they threw away their sacred thread and thus became Kulalupta or Kalita. Others say that they are not Kshatriyas, they entered Assam before the coming of the Vedic Aryans and thus they are non-Vedic Aryans.

According to some they were originally Buddhists. To others they were formerly priests of the Boros.

Regarding their original homeland and entry to Assam there are two views. It is generally believed that they came from the west by the route formed by the valleys of the Brahmaputra and the Ganges. The other view may be expressed in the language of Captain Neufville (1828), who stated: "The country to the eastward of Bhot and northward of Sadiya, extending on the plain beyond the mountains is said to be possessed by a powerful nation called Kalitas or Kultas, who are described as having attained to a high degree of advancement and civilization equal to any of the nations of the East" (c.f. Barua 1951).

The Kalitas are divided into two main sub-divisions, namely, Bar Kalita and Saru Kalita. Again, on the basis of the profession followed by some of them, several occupational sub-castes, which, however, are not endogamous, may be recognized. Some of these are Kahar Kalita, Kumar Kalita, Mali Kalita, Nat Kalita, Bez Kalita, etc.

The Kayasthas, popularly known as the 'Kaith' are mainly found in Lower Assam. They Wear sacred thread. They claim to be the descendants of those Kayasthas who were given settlements by the King Durlov Narayan. Their number is comparatively small. Traditionally, the Baishya is a trader caste. But the Assamese Baishyas are mostly agriculturist.

The Keot is another agricultural caste, which belongs to the 'Sudir' fold. There are two broad divisions of the Keot, namely, Halwa Keot and Jalwa Keot. The Halwa Keots belong to the general caste, while the Jalwa Keots (Jalkeot) are included in the Scheduled Caste category. The Keots are distributed in different parts of the Brahmaputra valley.

Some of the important Assamese Scheduled Castes are the Hira, Kaibarta, Jalkeot, Bania, Namasudra, etc. The Hiras are potters. They make pottery with hand without using potter's wheel. Only the female section of the caste is found to be engaged in manufacturing vessels. However, the male members participate in other activities, for example, by fetching raw materials, in baking the vessels, selling the products, etc. The Hiras are mostly met with in Lower and Middle Assam.

The traditional occupation of the Kaibarta is fishing. Some are boatmen. Many of them are agriculturist. They are distributed all over Assam. They prefer to live on river banks or near to sources of water. The Jalkeot are also fishermen.

The Kumar caste is included in the list of the Other Backward Classes (OBC). They form a potter caste. They manufacture earthen vessels with the help of wheel, unlike the Hiras. They are found in different parts of Assam. The Jogis, also known as the Naths, belong to the OBC. They are met with different regions of Assam. The Marias, a section of the Assamese Muslims, also belong to the OBC group. The Ahoms, Moram and Mataks are also members of the OBC.

The Rajbanshis, who are referred to as Koch also, can be cited as excellent example of tribe-caste continuum not only in terms of socio-cultural aspects but also in respect of certain biological process. According to the Census Report of 1891 "in Assam Rajbanshis are mainly persons of Koch and Mech tribes who have assumed this name on conversion to Hinduism". Persons of other tribes, e.g., Rabha, Kachari, Garo, Karbi, Tiwa, etc., also can become Koch or Rajbanshi after conversion to Hinduism. They are allotted a place in the caste-fold of the Hindu society. Hence, the Rajbanshi are of Mongoloid origin, and are somewhat heterogeneans. It is difficult to ascertain when did this process of conversion start. The process is still going on. The Rajbanshis are recognized as an Other Backward Class by the government. They will be discussed again under different context.

In addition to these population groups of Assam, several other populations also live in Assam. Assam is a state of India. Therefore. it is quite natural that in Assam there will be certain populations, which have come in different times from different parts of India. They migrated to Assam mostly for economic reasons. This sort of migration started mainly with the coming of the British after the fall of the Ahom rule. Some of them have become Assamese and many of them have been Assamized. These people are part and parcel of the Assamese society. Others, however, are maintaining their own socio-cultural identities.

The other divisions include two categories of people. One is in Assam for its own economic benefit. The members of this category are least concerned with Assam's interest so long as they are not directly affected. They have their second foot in their respective home states. In time of crisis in Assam, they can leave for their home states at any moment. This may affect their economy to a certain extent but not vitally. Therefore, this section of people could leave Assam without any second thought during the last Chinese aggression.

The members of the second category, though they have no second footing in their own states, are in Assam physically, but their mind and soul are in their own state. They know more about their own state than of Assam. They have never tried to be acquainted with the Assamese way of life, not to speak of accepting, following or even participating in it. They are always guided by the so-called leaders of their own state. Assam has not been benefitted in any way by the presence of these people. On the other hand, sometimes they do not hesitate to work against the interest of Assam. In this context it should clearly be stated that the employees of various organisations who are temporarily posted in Assam have not been taken into account in this discussion.

Language

The Assamese speak an Indo-Aryan language known as the Assamese, which has its root in the Sanskrit. However, the language had to pass through different stages of development in different times to assume its present form. In the course of its formation and development it has incorporated in it several words from different languages: Austric, Dravidian, Tibeto-Burman, etc., in addition to English, Arabic, Parsi, etc. The words from various linguistic families have enriched the Assamese vocabulary. Accordingly to 1971 census, 60.88 per cent of the total population of Assam speak Assamese language.

Many of the Assam tribes, who belong to Tibeto-Burman linguistic family, still speak their own respective languages of that language family. Others have forgotten their own dialect and have accepted Assemese as their mother tongue. The

Ahoms, who entered Assam in the early part of the thirteenth century, were speakers of the Thai language, a branch of the Siamese-Chinese linguistic family. Coming to Assam they gradually abandoned their original Thai language and accepted the Assamese language. There are some other small populations like the Tai Phake, Khamyang, Turung, Aiton, etc., who also belong to the same linguistic family. They have preserved their own languages.

A small number of the Khasis are also met with, in some parts of Assam. The language of the Khasis is entirely different from that of the Tibeto-Burman as well as Indo-Aryans. They speak Austroasiatic language. Again, though many of the population groups who work in the tea gardens speak their own dialect among themselves, yet they communicate with their counterparts in the gardens as well as other people through the Assamese language (Chah Bagichar Asomia).

Religion

According to the 1991 census 67.13 per cent of the people of Assam are Hindu. The Muslims constitute 28.43 per cent of the total population. The Christian, Sikh, Buddhist and Jain form 3.32 per cent, 0.07 per cent, 0.29 per cent and 0.09 per cent respectively. (Table 2)

Table 2 : Religious Groups of Assam

Religious Group	*Population*	*Percentage*
Hindus	15,047,293	67.13
Muslims	6,373,204	28.43
Sikhs	16,492	0.07
Christians	744,367	3.32
Buddhists	64,008	0.29
Jains	20,645	0.09

Source : Census of India, 1991.

In some of the districts of Upper Assam, there are certain small populations which are Buddhist by religion. They are the Khamyang, Aiton, Tai Phake, Turung, Duania etc., living in small pockets surrounded by people of other religions. They are faithfully following their own religion.

The Sikhs include two categories, one, the Punjabi Sikhs who came in recent years for various purposes, and the other, the Assamese Sikhs. The majority of the Assamese Sikhs are concentrated in a village called Borkhola in Nagaon district. Some of them live in Darrang district also. They are the descendants of those Sikh soldiers who came from the Punjab to help one of the Ahom rulers to fight against the Burmese invaders. After the war many soldiers preferred to settle in Assam permanently. They married local girls, and in due course one religious community came into being.

History tells that Assam came into contact with the Muslims for the first time in the early part of the thirteenth century when Muhammad bin Bakhtiyar Khilji, a Muslim general of Kutubuddin led a Turkish army to this region. Following him, on several occasions other Muslim invaders came to Assam. Every time they were defeated. It may, perhaps, be assumed that a few Muslim soldiers preferred to live in Assam instead of going back with their defeated leaders. In the middle of the sixteenth century a Muslim army, commanded by Turbak invaded Assam. Turbak was defeated and killed in the battle-field. Some of his soldiers were captured and taken as prisoners by the Ahom King. They were given settlement in different parts of Assam. These Muslims took working on brass metal. This occupation is still followed by many of their descendants. They are known as the Marias (Das and Ali, 1984).

A Muslim saint Hazarat Shah Milan by name, but popularly known as Azan Fakir came to Assam in the middle of the seventeenth century. He was a Syed. He promoted and stabilized Islam in Assam.

Many local people were converted to Islam because of his influence. However, many conversions generally took place through marriage, because the Muslim soldiers did not bring their wives with them and hence, they had to marry local girls. Again, the Ahom kings encouraged certain Muslim artisan families to migrate to Assam to take part in different activities. Thus, there were slow incorporation of Muslim into Assam in small numbers over a long period of time. In this way the traditional Assamese Muslim community, which gradually came into being includes the descendants of the Muslim soldiers, the artisan families, the Muslim preachers and the local converts. All these Assamese Muslims belong to the Sunni sect of Islam.

At various socio-cultural levels the Assamese Hindus and Muslims interact freely. Many socio-cultural elements, more particularly at folk-level, of the Assamese Hindus and Muslims are very similar. This is perhaps, as has already been mentioned, because conversion mainly took place through marriage and there was no large scale migration of Muslims to Assam in the past. They came in small numbers and time to time, and gradually became part of the greater Assamese community. Influence of Hindu caste system on the Assamese Muslims is indicated in their social organisation. They have three broad 'caste like' divisions, namely, the Syeds, who claim to be the descendants of Prophet Muhammad; the Sheikhs, who form the major bulk of the population; and the Marias, the descendants of the captured

Muslim soldiers. The Syeds claim to occupy the highest social status. Next to them come the Sheikhs to be followed by the Marias (Ali 1974; 1979; 1985).

Christianity spread with the coming of the British and American missionaries. However, it is mostly confined to the tribal people, more particularly the hill tribes now inhabiting the adjoining states. Most of the Assam tribes, more particularly of the plains, are Hindu or Hinduised, though many of them practise their own religions.

Immigration

Assam witnessed a series of immigration in the modern time. Reference has already been made to the labourers in the tea-gardens. With the opening of the gardens in the beginning of the second half of the 19th century, labourers, to work in the gardens were brought from Bihar, Orissa, Madhya Pradesh, etc. By 1901 the total number became about 6,54,000. The number went on increasing till 1941, when mass importation of labour was stopped. Even then in natural course their number increased. Many labourers left the tea estates and settled down as farmers in government wastelands or plot provided by the garden authorities. They are referred to a ex-tea-garden-workers. Tea garden and ex-tea garden workers form a heterogeneous people, as they came from different regions and belong to different ethnic groups. But in Assam they are regarded as forming one unit.

In recent years a large number of people from other parts of India having different ethnic identities have come to Assam to settle permanently. This includes people of various linguistic and cultural groups. Moreover, many Nepalis have also come from the neighbouring country Nepal. In 1951 the total number of the Nepali population was 1,25,000 which rose to about 2,00,000 in 1961. It can be assumed that by 1971 it became about 3,00,000. Many of the Nepalis have adopted Assamese as their mother tongue, and hence they are not included under 'Nepali'. Most of the Nepalis came to Assam as livestock farmers, mostly cattle and buffaloes; but later on they took up farming of land also as a profession and gradually became permanent settlers.

When Assam came under the British rule, the British brought with them some Bengalees to serve them and to help them in different matters. These Bengalees encouraged other Bengalees to follow them. Mostly for the economic reason they preferred to do so and still they are doing that. They are found in varied professions, from petty traders and doing odd jobs to holding high government and non-government offices.

Immigration to Assam from East Bengal (East

Pakistan, Bangladesh) is going on unabted since the beginning of the 20th century. The fertile land of Assam attracted the East Bengalee (mostly Muslim) farmers. Immigration started. Firstly, they established settlement in Goalpara district, mostly in the 'Char' lands and reserved forests, and then fanned out like bees to other parts of the state. By 1931 their total number became about 5,75,000. Most of them came from one district of Bengal, called Mymenshing, and therefore they are sometimes referred to as 'Mymenshingia'. From 1931 they got political patronage and as a result the process was intensified. The number of Muslims in Assam started rising remarkably, not because of conversion or high birth rate, but because of such unabated immigration. The number of original Assamese Muslims has become insignificant in comparison to that of the immigrant Muslims.

Since the partition of India the influx of Hindu refugees to Assam from East Pakistan started and it is still continuing. As per the 1951 census their number was about 2,75,000. By April 1968 the number increased to about 10,68,500. Assam experienced another mass immigration of people from the same region during the Bangladesh war of 1971. Both Hindus and Muslims started moving to Assam. Some of the refugees belong to middle-class urban minded people, who have settled in and around the towns being engaged in small trades and taking jobs of varied nature, while others are cultivators and they have penetrated into the rural areas (data on Immigration have been taken from Chaudhuri, 1982).

These immigrations, more specifically from East Bengal, East Pakistan, and Bangladesh, have created a big problem to the people of Assam. The demographic picture of Assam has completely been changed. Long back in 1931, Mullan the then Census Superintendent wrote in the census report, "This influx of immigrants is likely to alter permanently the whole future of Assam and to destroy more surely than the Burmese invaders of 1820, the whole structure of Assamese culture and civilization." What Mullan predicted about seventy years back has become the reality today. The Assamese people are going to become minority in their own homeland. Therefore, the people of Assam are making efforts by adopting different measures to safeguard the interest of the people and to preserve their socio-cultural identity.

Chapter 2
Race

Anthropologists' concept of race, their approach to classification of race and to the factors responsible for the formation of race etc., have greatly been changed during the last five decades, because of discoveries of certain new facts, advancement of scientific knowledge, advanced methodology, use of sophisticated apparatus and so forth. Some anthropologists are not even willing to recognize the existence of classical racial units. Their whole approach can be termed as non-racial. The racial classifications are made taking into account several racial criteria of different natures as the bases. As many of these criteria are not fixed qualities and are changeable to different forms under different conditions and the factors along with the related processes responsible for such phenomena are known to the modern anthropologists, they are hesitant to give any importance to such criteria. Under these circumstances, the importance of studying racial elements in a country in the present time has obviously been diminished. But at the same time in such racial studies, the classical approach cannot be totally ignored. One must first understand the existing basic facts and then can go for explanations. Here lies the importance of the classical approach. Anyway, in the present study the classical or conventional approach will be followed to discuss the racial elements in the people of Assam and then reference will be made to certain processes currently involved in certain populations of this region to evaluate the different situations which deserve indepth study of special nature.

Race is a concept. The term race is used in different senses by scientists, politicians, historians and the like. But the UNESCO (United Nations Educational, Scientific and Cultural Organization) issued a statement on race in 1950 where it has clearly been mentioned that the "concept of race is unanimously regarded by anthropologists as a classificatory device providing a zoological frame within which the various groups of mankind may be arranged and by means of which studies of evolutionary process can be facilitated." The term race has been defined as "a group or population characterized by some concentrations, relative as to frequency and distribution, of hereditary particles (genes) or physical characters, which appear, fluctuate, and often disappear in the course of time by reason of geographical and/or cultural isolation." It is further stated that "national, religious, geographic, linguistic, cultural groups do not necessarily coincide with racial group and the cultural traits of such groups have no demonstrated genetic connection with racial traits." In the opinion of the UNESCO it is better to use the term 'ethnic group' instead of 'race'. This will remove certain wrong notions connected with race. It is always desirable to understand fully this anthropological concept of race and the biological aspects of this while dealing with that racial or ethnic elements of any geographic region or political unit.

Racial Criteria

Racial groups are described taking into account certain biological traits, which are usually referred to as racial criteria. Three broad categories of such racial criteria may be made. *Firstly*, some common variable characters, which may be termed as morphological traits, and which are mostly polygenic in nature and hence, their hereditary mechanisms are not simple and are not perfectly known. Some such morphological traits can be easily observed with naked eye or with the aids of certain devices. These include skin colour, hair form, hair texture, eyebrows, malar prominence, ear lobe, etc. On the other hand, some morphological traits like total facial height, head length, head breadth, nasal height, nasal breadth, different body segments, are described by taking some specific measurements methodically with the help of instruments designed for the purpose. *Secondly*, some common physiological traits, the genetic background and hereditary processes of which are well-established. Some such traits are ABO blood group, MN blood type, Rh blood factor and so forth. *Thirdly*, some rare traits, which occur in low frequencies in human populations, for example, colour blindness, albinism, etc.; or, it may be completely absent in one population, while another may exhibit it in considerable numbers. The hereditary mechanisms of such traits are fairly well known.

A racial criteria is expected to fulfil certain conditions, for example, it should be non-adaptive, that means, natural selection should not play very effective role; a criterion should not easily be modified to a great extent by environmental factors; a trait must be objective or in other words it must be very clearly defined so that different investigators do not show individual variation in recording and classifying the concerned trait; a criterion should be controlled by known genetic process, and more the mechanism simple, is always better; and a high rate of mutation should not alter frequently the nature of the traits, so that the frequency of such trait in a population does not show considerable variations from time to time.

The racial elements in the population of Assam will be examined taking into account mostly different morphological traits, more particularly, stature, head form, face form, nose form, hair form etc., though occasionally references will be made to ABO blood groups also. At one time much importance was given on these traits, because it was thought that these are very dependable criteria as these do not change easily. But now their importance has greatly been diminished. Several works have demonstrated that stature easily undergoes changes under different ecological conditions. Cultural factors have also effect on stature. Moreover, in case of such characters we know about their phenotypic expressions only. Populations are described by giving the frequencies of the different phenotypes, for example, in case of head, the percentage of brachycephals (broad-headed), mesocephals (medium-headed), dolichocephals (long-headed), etc., and also mentioning the mean values of such traits as shown by the populations. Again, with regard to descriptive traits, in many cases, subjectivity cannot be totally avoided.

The second category of the traits have many more advantages over the first one. For example, in most of the cases the genes involved in producing a trait is known. Hence, alongwith giving the percentile occurrences of the phenotypes, the frequencies of genes can also be calculated by applying appropriate statistical formulae. Many such traits also are, however, adaptive, that is, subjected to selection. Some such genetic markers are blood groups (ABO, Rh, MNSs, etc.), taste sensitivity to phenylthiocarbamide (PTC) and so forth. In the present context we can perhaps ignore the third category and also the mutation factor.

This does not necessarily mean that now the time has come to completely ignore the morphological traits. On the contrary, in traditional physical anthropology even now normal morphological variables constitute the central field of study. Therefore, two eminent physical anthropologists have rightly remarked that these morphological traits "constitute a whole field of human variation in size and shape, furthermore involving modification by environment as well as relationship and differentiation of populations (Oliver and Howells, 1957).

Racial Classification

The human figures, painted by using different colours, in Egyptian royal tombs of the XVII to the XXI dynasties, give an indication that from the ancient times, population variation in respect of skin colour was marked by the people. The Egyptians used four different colours to represent four varieties of human groups. In 200 BC the Chinese distinguished five human groups on the basis of skin colour.

During the 17th century Bernier travelled through different parts of the Old World, when he came across various human populations, which he classified into four groups in 1684 according to their physical features. This may be regarded as the first attempt to classify human populations. The second attempt was made by Bradley in 1721. He made three major groups, namely, White, Negro and Intermediate (Mulatto) on the basis of skin colour. In this classification there is no mention of the yellow (Mongoloid) people. But perhaps the credit should be given to Carl Linnaeus (1707 — 1778 A.D), a Swedish naturalist, for his making a systematic classification of the human species, which he named Homo sapiens. His four divisions of Homo sapiens are as follows:

1. Homo americanus (American Indian) : They are tenacious, contended and free, and are ruled by custom.
2. Home europaeus : They are characterized by light, lively and inventive nature, and are ruled by rites.
3. Homo asiaticus : They are stern, haughty andstingy, and are ruled by opinion.
4. Homo afer (African) : They are by nature

cunning, slow and negligent, and are ruled by caprice.

It may be noted that Linnaeus classification is based on certain mental traits, and not on physical features.

In 1775, a German scientist, Blumenbach by name, identified five varieties of man, which are:

1. Caucasian or White
2. Mongolian or Yellow
3. Ethiopian or Black
4. American or Red
5. Malayan or Brown

Each one of these was called 'race', a term first coined by a French scientist named Buffon. It may be noted that Blumenbach classified human species taken into account a single biological treat, i.e., the skin colour.

During the 19th century several scholars like Pickering (1848), Huxley (1870), Topinard (1885), Quatrafages (1889), Deniker (1889) proposed different classifications of mankind. In course of time more and more physical traits were taken into consideration and new methods were employed to classify human races.

In 1923 Dixon took into account three indices, namely, cephalic index, length-height index, and nasal index, for classification of human races. In 1924 Haddon proposed a classification of mankind using hair form as the primary trait, and stature, cephalic index and nasal index as secondary traits.

Hooton, an American anthropologist, in 1931 identified three primary races, namely, White (Caucasoid), Negroid and Mongoloid, with several secondary, composite and sub-races. He modified his classification in 1947. On the other hand, Eickstedt (1934), a German anthropologist, recognized three basic races; Europoid, Mongoloid and Negroid with eighteen sub-races, three collateral races, even collateral sub-races and three intermediate forms. According to Vallois, a French anthropologist, there are four major races, namely, Australoid, Black, Yellow and White, each having certain sub-races. There are others also who attempted to classify human races.

Under 'racial criteria' it has been said that certain genetic markers in blood, for example, ABO blood groups, MN blood type, RH factor, etc., are also used in classifying racial groups. Scientists like Ottenberg, Synder, Lahovary, Weiner and Boyd on the basis of such genetic traits divided the human races into different groups at different times. Here we may cast a glance on the classification proposed by Boyd in 1958, which is as follows:

I. European Group : (1) Early Europeans

(2)Lapps (3)North-West Europeans (4) Eastern and Central Europeans and (5)Mediterranean

II. African Group : (6) The African races excluding the inhabitants of North Africa, who belong to the European Group

III. Asian Group : (7) The Asian races (8) Indo-Dravidian

IV. American Group : (9) American Indians

V. Pacific Group : (10) Indonesian race (11) Melanesian race (12) Polynesian race

VI. Australian Group : (13) Australian aborigines

Through different anthropologists proposed different classifications of races at different times, yet in general it could be said that there are three major races, namely, Caucasoid (White), Mongoloid (Yellow) and Negroid (Black). According to some anthropologists there are four major races, the fourth being the Australoid. Others prefer to include the Australoid under the Caucasoid calling them by the name Archaic Caucasoid. Each of the major races can be divided into certain groups and subgroups. For example:

The Negroid has two broad divisions. One, the African Negro and the other, the Oceanic Negro. The African Negroes are further divided into five subgroups, namely, the True Negroes, Nilotic

Negroes or Nilote, Bantu-speaking Negroes or Bantu, Bushmen-Hottentot and the Negrillo. The Oceanic Negroes include the Negritos, both Asiatic and Oceanic, and the Melanesians and Papuans.

The Mongoloids may be divided into four main sub-divisions according to their geographical distribution. These are: the Classic or Central Mongoloids, the Arctic or Northern Mongoloids or Eskimoids, the Southern or Indo-Malayan Mongoloids and the American-Indians.

Unlike the Negroids and the Mongoloids, the Caucasoids cannot be divided into certain distinct sub-divisions. They include a large number of ethnic groups with diverse racial characteristics. Some of the important groups are: the Mediterranean having three subdivisions, viz., Classic Mediterranean, Atlanto-Mediterranean and Indo-Afghan Mediterranean, the Alpine, the Nordic, the Armenoid, the Dinaric (Adriatic or Illyrian), the Keltic, the East Baltic, the Indo-Dravidian, the Ainu, etc.

The Australian aborigines and the Pre-Dravidians belong to the Australoids.

In the next chapter an attempt will be made to find out which of these races and their subgroups have contributed racial elements towards the formation of the people of Assam.

Chapter 3
Racial Elements in Assam

Sources of Information

The Indo-Aryans entering into India met several groups of which two were easily distinguishable from one another and also from the Indo-Aryans. One of them is the Nishada and the other one is the Kirata. In ancient Sanskrit literature the Nishada have been described as short-statured, dark-complexioned people. They had long head and dark wavy head hair. In the *Bhagavata Purana* there is a nice description of the physical features of the Nishada, which is as follows : "black like crow, very low statured, short armed, having high cheek bones, low tipped nose, red eyes and copper coloured hair" (translated by S.S. Sarkar, 1962). Some anthropologists have used this term Nishada to denote the Australoids. Sporadic references to some aspects of physical features of the Kirata are also found in ancient literature. For example, in the *Ramayana* their skin colour has been described as 'shining like gold.' In the

Mahabharata and also in the *Kalika Purana*, references have been made to their yellow skin colour. Thus, the dark-skinned Nishadas were very much different from the yellowish-skinned Kiratas. One can have some idea about the geographical distribution of the Kiratas from the *Vishnu Purana* wherein it is stated that "(India) is in the middle, according to the division (of the world) with the Brahmanas, Kshatriyas, Vaishyas and Shudras; in the east (of India) are the Kiratas and to the west are the Yavanas" (translated by S.K. Chatterjee, 1951). Thus, the various ancient literature provide certain information on the physical features of different populations. Moreover, a careful scrutiny of the literatures gives an idea about the antiquity of the various populations groups, their geographical distribution and migration in different times on which a glance will be cast in proper place.

In addition to such written records, unwritten legends, folktales, traditional stories etc., prevalent among different populations groups can also be used as source materials to understand certain facts. Many of the Assam tribes have respectfully preserved such traditional stories since long past and feel proud to narrate those to establish their antiquity, ancestors, routes of migration, contact with other populationss and the like. A few such stories will be examined in due course to trace the routes of migration of some of the populations groups.

Language is a very dependable evidence to demonstrate contact in ancient times among various populationss. A language changes or evolves in course of time on account of various factors, one being incorporation of new words from other languages through contact. Penetration of words from one linguistic group to another, their retention, changes of form through ages, etc, reveal very important information which can carefully and meaningfully be utilized in understanding different aspects of ethnic composition.

The type of man that lived in Assam in the prehistoric past is still a matter of conjecture in the absence of adequate information. No human or humanoid skeletal remains of prehistoric time have yet been unearthed from any part of this region. However, some Palaeolithic tools and a large number of neoliothic implements alongwith other findings have been reported by different scholars from time to time, which clearly throws some lights on the subject of men and culture of the prehistoric period of Assam.

The fifth and the most authentic source for examination to determine the racial elements that have entered into the populations of Assam is provided by the physical anthropological materials reported by various workers at different times. The history of research in physical anthropology in

Assam dates back to the beginning of the 20th century, when Waddell (1901) took anthropometric measurements on 564 individuals belonging to 33 different populationss of the Brahmaputra valley. He published the individual measurements alongwith an introductory ethnographic note to each of the populationss measured. Fifteen years later, Brown and Kemp (1915) measured 84 male and 10 female Abors. Again, in 1921 Hutton reported anthropometric data on 234 individuals belonging to 7 Naga tribes. He was followed by Dixon (1922) to collect anthropometric data on 25 Khasi, 10 Angami Naga and 8 Sema Naga. Dixon analysed his data to throw some light on the racial history of Assam. A new set of data on the Sema and Angami Naga was added by Singh in 1935. Shaw (1929) and T.C. Das (1945) studied the anthropometric traits of the Thado Kuki and Purum Kuki respectively, each measuring 60 individuals from each of the populationss. The Khasi tribe was studied from this angle by three different anthropologists, namely, Guha (1935), Raychoudhury (1935) and Bowles (1943). In 1938 Dutta provided scanty information on anthropometric character of several castes of Assam. Guha and Basu (1931) published a report on the human relics recovered by the Naga Hills expedition for the abolition of human sacrifice, during 1926-27. To these may be added three sets of data on ABO blood groups reported by Mitra (1936) from among the Assamese of the plains, Angami Naga and Lushai tribe; two sets of Khasi data, one by Basu (1938) and the other by Macfarlance (1941); and two sets of Naga data reported by the British Association (1939).

These were the important materials on physical anthropology of the people of Northeast India till 1947. The situation started changing from 1947 or from the beginning of the second half of the 20th Century. The year 1947 is very important *firstly*, because India won independence and, *secondly*, a teaching department of anthropology for the first time was opened in the Cotton College, Guwahati in that year. Anyway, the period between 1901 and 1950 may be regarded as the 'Initial Stage' of research in physical anthropology in Northeast India. The next stage began from 1951 and till now it is continuing. This stage may be called 'Data Generating' or 'Reporting Stage'. During this period reports on physical anthropological aspects of the people started pouring through the efforts of individual workers and also of team of researchers. As a result at the moment there are several studies on physical anthropology of the different populations of Assam. A systematic examination of these materials can give valuable information on the racial elements in the people of Assam.

A Glance on India

Before making an attempt to examine the racial

elements in Assam, perhaps it will be better to cast a glance on India in general and northeast India in particular.

Several classifications of the people of India have been proposed by several anthropologists like Risley (1915), Giufrida-Ruggeri (1921), Eickstedt (1934), Guha (1935), Sarkar (1962) since the early part of the 20th century, of which the classification done by B.S. Guha got wider publicity and more recognition, because it was a some sort of official document and hence was very easily available to all. Whoever speaks of racial types in India, always refers to Guha's classification. We too, do not propose to make any marked deviation from such practice and accept this as the main one, though references will also be made to other's work, especially to that of S.S. Sarkar. Even then let us look at the classifications made by others also.

Risley divided the people of India into the following types:

(a) Turko-Iranian
(b) Indo-Aryan
(c) Scythio-Dravidian
(d) Aryo-Dravidian or Hindustani type
(e) Monglo-Dravidian or Bengali type
(f) Mongoloid
(g) Dravidian

Guifrida-Ruggeri observed the following ethnic

stratification in India :

(a) Negritos
(b) Pre-Dravidians (Australoid, Veddaic)
(c) Dravidians
(d) Tall dolichocephalic (Mesocephalic?) elements
(e) Dolichocephalic Aryans (Homo Indo-europeaus dolichomorphus)
(f) Brachycephalic leucoderms (Homo Indo-europeaus brachymorphus)

Eickstedt classified the people of India into four main divisions, namely:

1. Weddid or Ancient Indians
   (a) Gondid
   (b) Malid
2. Melanid or Black Indians
   (a) Southern Melanid
   (b) Kolid
3. Indid or New Indians
   (a) Gracile Indid
   (b) North Indid
4. Palae-Mongoloid

Guha identified six main racial types with nine sub-types in the populations of India. These are:

1. Negrito
2. Proto-Australoid
3. Mongoloid
   (a) Palae-Mongoloid divided into (i) long-headed and (ii) broad-headed

(b) Tibeto-Mongoloid

4. Mediterranean
   (a) Palae-Mediterranean
   (b) Mediterranean
   (c) Oriental type
5. Western Brachycephal
   (a) Alpinoid
   (b) Dinaric
   (c) Armenoid
6. Nordic

Sarkar observed the following six racial elements in the populations of India

1. Australoid
2. Indo-Aryan
3. Irano-Scythian
4. Mundari-Speaker
5. Far-Eastern (Malay-Polynenian)
6. Mongolian

To these may be added the opinion of Majumder (1965): "The Pre-Dravidians, the Dravidians (brunette dolichocephals), the Indo-Aryans (fair dolichocephals), the Indo-Alpines (brachycephals) and the Mongolians constitute the racial elements in the populations of India".

Assam : Earlier Studies

R.B. Dixon, analysing the anthropometric data collected by him from the then Assam identified four main types with intermediaries on the basis of head form and nose form. These are:

Brachycephalic-leptorrhine, Brachycephalic-platyrrhine, Dolichocephalic-leptorrhine and Dolichocephalic-platyrhine. According to him the Dolichocephalic-platyrrhine type represent the aboriginal Negroids who were assimilated by the Brachycephalic-platyrrhine. He writes "this type represents the western expansion of that type which forms the fundamental stratum among the populations of southern China and much of south-eastern Asia and the Malay Archepelago. It brought with it the ancestral form of Mon-Khmer speech." On the other hand the Brachycephalic-leptorrhine type "appears to represent the southern extension of a great area, characterised by this factor, which includes most of Central Asia and the Great Plateaus, Northern China, and much of the northeastern portion of the Continent, and as a type shows very close relationship with the Alpine, so widely spread in Central and Western Europe." At a much later date the Aryan immigrants brought the Dolichocephalic-leptorrhine type of Bengal and Assam through the Gangetic valley. Thus, Dixon is inclined to believe that the earliest inhabitants of Assam were of Negroid type.

A.C. Haddon also considered head form and nose form in isolating the racial types in the populations of the then Assam. He identified seven ethnic elements, which are as follows:

(1) Dolichocephalic-platyrrhine type (Pre-

Dravidians): This element is strong among the Khasi, Kuki, Manipuri, Kachari, etc. It occurs in weaker form among the Naga tribes.

(2) Dolichocephalic-mesorrhine type (Nesiot element): It is noticed among the Naga tribes and other hill tribes.

(3) Mesocephalic-platyrrhine type : "It is noticed among the Khasi and appears to have the same relative importance in Chota Nagpur, and in Burma among the Southern Chin, Palaung and Burmese, and a greater among the Kachin."

(4) Mesocephalic-mesorrhine type : Outside Assam it occurs among the Lepcha and Murmi and in certain castes of Bengal and Bihar.

(5) Brachycephalic-leptorrhine type : It came from the north and is related to the Eurasiatic group.

(6) Brachycephalic-platyrrhine type : It is a variety of the Pareoean type.

(7) Dolichocephalic-leptorrhine type : This element came from India, i.e., from western direction.

Haddon's analyses clearly indicate that he did not find any Negrito strains in Assam. Dixon called the Dolichocephalic-platyrrhine type as the aboriginal Negroid, while to Haddon this type represents the Pre-Dravidians.

Barua (1936) examined the available

anthropological materials to arrive at certain conclusion regarding race and race movements in northeast India. Hutton (1931) also dealt with some aspects of this subject. Their works will be referred to in appropriate places.

Negrito Element in Assam

According to Guha the Negritos were the first to come to India and they are the true autocthones of India. Hutton also holds the same view that the earliest inhabitants of India were probably of the Negrito race, and this element formed one of the earliest strains in the inhabitants of the hills of Assam. Mills (1935) also wrote that "inhabitants of the mountains of Assam were almost certainly Negritos, little dark men with curly hair .... It was probably they who made the little stone celts, which are frequently found in the hills." The assessments of the scholars like Guha, Hutton, Mills as regards the presence of Negrito element in Assam is based on hair form and certain cultural elements. They observed frizzly form of head hair, the so-called Negrito feature, among a handful of Naga people. But with regard to anthro- pometric traits among the Nagas, nobody mentioned the occurrence of Negrito strains in them. G. Olivier (1958) remarked that among the Nagas "none of the subjects showed any Negritoid characteristics." Suri (1986) also did not report any Negrito trait from among the Angami Nagas. S.K. Chatterjee

(1951) also believes that the Negritos are the first inhabitants of India. He wrote "First we have in prehistoric times, the arrival of the Negritos, a dwarfish Negriod of Negro-like people, from Africa.... traces of them being found as far east as Assam among the Nagas, and remnants of them are found in South India among a few wild tribes."

In this context it may be mentioned that the opinions differ as regards the contribution of the Negritos towards the formation of the basic substratum of the populations of the mainland on India. However, nobody can deny that the Andamanese who live in Andaman islands, are one of the true representatives of the Negrito. But as Risley rightly remarked "they have had no share in the making of the Indian populations." Haddon gave a general description of the Andamanese. They are very short-statured, dark-skinned, woolly-haired and brachycephalic people. De Quatrafeges has also described the Negritos as brachycephalic. But the Angamis measured by Hutton are in average mesocephalic. The Dolichocephalic-platyrrhine type of Dixon, who according to him represents the aboriginal Negroid type of Assam are not brachycephalic. Hutton observed sporadic occurrence of woolly hair among the Angami Nagas. Hair form is one of the several racial criteria though Guha put undue emphasis on it. Moreover, in describing hair form the terms woolly and frizzly were used indiscriminately, which is not desirable from the scientific point of view, because there is difference between genetic feature of frizzly hair of the Negroes and ordinary frizzly hair. Besides sporadic occurrence of woolly or frizzly hair in certain families can, by no means support the existence of a Negrito strain in the basic substratum of a particular populations. The development of modern scientific concept does not encourage one to accept such hypothesis. However, one must not forget that Guha proposed his classification in 1931, when the science of human genetics did not develop to a great extent. L.A.K. Iyer (1936) also mentioned the form of head hair as a Negrito element in certain populations of South India. Majumder wrote on Iyer's observation : "no specific mention has been made of the incidence of this character and no microscopic examination of hair is available to support Iyer's evidence." In a discussion on Negrito element in India very often mention is made of a south Indian tribe called the Kadars, which according to Guha, Ehrenfels, etc., show Negrito element, to be more specific woolly or frizzly hair. Ehrenfels published a few photographs of woolly-haired Kadars to establish his view. But in 1959 Sarkar and his colleagues made a detailed study of several physical anthropological traits like anthropometry, ABO blood groups, dermatoglyphics, somatoscopy, hair form of the Kadars and came to the conclusion that no Negrito elements are found in them. The Kadars are very much like the other Australoid tribes of south India, and they may very well be listed along with the Paniyan, Kannikar, etc., as one of the Australoid tribes.

Sarkar and Majumder independently discussed in details the Negrito problem in India and both of them discarded the idea that the Negritos were the earliest inhabitants of India. However, it cannot be denied that Negroid elements are observed in some coastal parts of India, but this element infiltrated into these regions during the eighth to tenth century A.D., and hence it cannot contribute its share to the basic substratum of the populations on India. The same observation is applicable to Assam as well. Under these circumstances, it can be said that till now there is no evidence to confirm the views expressed by some scholars that Negrito element at one time spread to the boundary of modern Assam.

Australoid Element in Assam

According to Guha, the Negritos are the earliest inhabitants of India, while Risley expressed the view that the first comers are the Dravidians. On the other hand Sarkar, Majumder and others are of the opinion that the Australoids are the autocthonous people of India. The Australoids are called by different names by different scholars.

Ruggeri called them Australo-Veddaic. Ecikstedt used the term Weddid (Veddid) because of their similarities with the Veddas of Sri Lanka in respect of physical features. Perhaps Lapicque was the first to use the term Pre-Dravidian. Haddon too used this term .The term Proto-Australoid was perhaps first coined by Dixon, and Guha and Sewell accepted this. Chanḍa, however, was in favour of preserving the ancient Sanskrit name the Nishada. Sarkar first accepted the term Veddid, but latre on he preferred to call them by the name Australoid. Here, this term, that is Australoid will be used.

Physical Features

A general description of the physical features of the Australoids can be given as follows: Hair is black, coarse and wavy or slightly curly in form. They are dark-skinned. Head is very long (dolichocephalic) with slightly retreating forehead and prominent brow-ridges. Their nose is very broad (platyrrhine) and depressed at the root. They are short-statured people. Their body is of delicately built.

Opinion differs as regards the genetic relationship of the Australoids with certain fossil types. Whatever that might be, most of the anthropologists believe that the Australoids represent a very ancient type of man. As a matter of fact some anthropologists prefer to call them by the name Archaic Caucasoid, and on account of their similarities in respect of many physical features with the Caucasoids mark them as sub-divisions of the Caucasoid, a major race of mankind.

Prehistoric India

As regards presence of the Australoid elements in prehistoric India, it may be pointed out that the Australoid type of crania have been unearthed from the Indus Valley sites, which represents a civilization that flourished during 3250 and 2750 B.C., approximately. Sewell and Guha (1931) collected from Mohenjodaro three crania, which according to them are of Proto-Australoid type. In Harappa, a cemetery with two layers of burials representing two distinct racial types have been identified. The layer has yielded skeletal materials having affinities with the Australoids, and are very similar to those collected from Mohenjodaro. Analysing the skeletal materials found in ancient Baluchistan, Sind and the Punjab, Sarkar (1964) has opined that "an autocthonous hyperdolichocephalic element represented by the Veddid or Australoid ethnic strain appears to be at the base of the Indus Valley people."

Several skeletal remains have been collected from the Iron Age site of Addittanallur of south

India. According to Guha some of them are of Australoid type. At Brahmagiri in Mysore Megalithic and Neolithic sites yielding skeletal remains having affinities with the Australoid type have been discovered. These are some of the examples of Australoid type found in different parts of India. Therefore, it can perhaps be said that a critical examination of the skeletal remains collected from different parts of India belonging to different periods of early time gives a clear indication of the presence of Australoid element in pre-historic and proto-historic India and that they were fairly distributed over the different regions of the country.

Contemporary India

Some of the present day important south Indian tribes having Australoid affinities and listed under the general term Pre-Dravidians are the Kadars of Cochin; the Paniyans of Malabar; Uralis, Kannikars and Mithuvan of Travancore; the Kurumba and Irula of the Nilgiris; and the Chenchus of Hyderabad. But it is not that the Australoid elements are very much restricted among these tribes only. On the contrary, these have penetrated to the other populationss of south and middle India. It has even spread to north and northeast. Sarkar has gone one step further to say that "the Australoid racial make-up is present among all the castes of India though its greatest concentration is found among the lower castes".

Majumder also subscribes to this view by saying that "the Australoid features are found throughout the length and breadth of Indian subcontinent".

Northeast India

As regards northeast India, Buxton as early as in 1935 wrote that "the basal type and probably the aboriginal is the Pre-Dravidian, but there is no exact data on this point at present. It is found among many of the isolated tribes". Perhaps one such isolated tribe is the Mros of Chittagong hills, among whom Mills observed "the almost entire absence of Mongolian traits in their features." Sarkar and Bhattacharjee (1958) called it an "old Veddid pocket." Haddon also "tentatively suggested an ancient dolichocephalic-platyrrhine (Pre-Dravidian) type which is strong among the Kuki, Khasi, Manipuri Kachari, etc". In 1972 the present writer came across a small populations near Imphal in Manipur the members of which appear to have certain Australoid traits in their physical features. Chatterjee (1951) observed "In Burma and Indo-China lived speakers of Austric (Austro-Asiatic) language, who are largely of the Proto-Australoid race from India." As has already been mentioned Dixon referred to a "previous aboriginal Negroid stratum". In all probabilities perhaps this element was not Negroid but Australoid. Because had there been assimilation of the Negrito race by the latter immigrants, one would have found in them at least certain characteristic Negrito traits, such as woolly hair and broad head of small size associated with very flat nose and very dark complexion. Guha and Basu studied certain crania of the Naga tribe, and identified two racial types which were termed as Group I and Group II. The latter was assigned to the Australoid.

Flatz and his colleagues (1972) made a survey on the occurrence of a haemoglobin variant called HbE. According to them "the pattern of distribution (of HbE) seen together with historical and cultural evidence, seems to permit the hypothesis that the entire area of Assam, northern Bengal and possibly parts of Nepal were inhabited in prehistoric time by a contingent of populations of matrilineal Austro-asiatic tribes among whom HbE spread after its introdution by migration from southeast Asia. The populations who migrated to the area subsequently acquired HbE by mixing with the original populations". However, in the context of the later findings this statement appears to require modification.

The data collected from various populations groups clearly indicate that the Austroasiatic background is unlikely to be the sole reason for high frequency of HbE in Assam. Deka et al (1988) observed : "with the centre of distribution of the gene in Northern Kampuchea and Northeast Thailand (Flatz, 1967) it is anomalous that the highest prevalence of HbE among the Tibeto-Burman of Assam is contradictory to the observations in Southeast Asia where among the Tibeto-Burman it is very low. It is difficult to explain these findings in the light of 'Austro-Asiatic hypothesis' which assumed a monofocal distribution of HbE. It may be speculated that HbE may have originated independently in more than one, at least in two locations resulting in two focal centre of distribution, one being Assam".

Assam

No doubt that the tribes of Assam are Mongoloid in origin. But among some Assam tribes there appear certain Australoid ethnic traits. A detailed study of several somatoscopic and anthropometric characters of the tribes like Boro, Kachari, Rabha, Garo, Tiwa, Karbi demonstrates occurrence of certain non-Mongoloid traits, which deserve explanation. There is no doubt that Caucasoid elements have liberally entered into the Mongoloid populations of Assam in considerable magnitude. (This aspect will be discussed in Chapter IV). But alongwith that Caucasoid traits, Australoid elements are also observed. When a particular populations is taken into consideration as a whole, such Australoid elements do not become conspicuous. On the other hand, careful study of some individuals clearly indicates existence of such traits in them.

When the Assam tribes were compared by the present writer (1970) with other Asiatic Mongoloids, it was found that the Assam tribes were shorter in stature and they had narrower heads. Though in general, many of the Assam tribes are characterised by mesocephalic head, dolichocephalic elements is equally strong in some of the tribes. A high percentage of them are dolichocephalic and a few of them exhibit hyperdolichocephalic (very long head) as well. As a matter of fact the tribes like the Rabha, Karbi, Garo have dolichocephalic mane. In this connection it may be mentioned that Buxton associated three people with dolichocephalic head form in India. They are : (i) the aboriginal peoples of India; (ii) the Dravidians; and (iii) the Indo-Aryans. Sarkar had also accepted this view. To him the aboriginal people of India show a basic Australoid strain in almost all of them in varying degrees, and secondly, the Dravidians appear to have evolved out of the above hyperdolichocephalic Australoids through various ecological changes and biological factors. It seems probable that the Australoids also contributed much of the dolichocephalic strain to the various Mongoloid tribes of northeast India in varying degrees, because the Indo-Aryans came to this region at a much later date to contribute their share to the basic substratum of the populations. The presence of very long head in the Rabha, Garo etc., may be reminiscent of the same.

In some caste populations also, certain Australoid elements are discernible, when individuals are observed minutely. In this context it may be recalled what Sarkar said about its occurrence in the castes of India, which have already been quoted. This has perhaps happened in case of some of the Assamese castes also.

On the basis of all these evidences it could perhaps be said that the Australoids were the first to come to Assam. It may be assumed that they left behind some genetic endowments. They came before the advent of the Mongoloids, who abserved partially or completely the old Australoid strains.

Though Australoid elements are observed among various groups of populations of Assam in varying degrees, yet at present there is no Australoid populations as such unlike other parts of India, more particularly south and central India. However, the labour force of the tea gardens (also ex-tea garden labourers) which is composed of heterogeneous elements, includes members of several tribes, for example, the Gond, Oraon, etc., showing distinct Australoid strains. Many of them have preserved their Australoid physical features. But it should not be forgotten that these Australoid populations migrated to Assam in modern period.

According to Chatterjee the Austric speech-family was associated with the Australoids and their descendants. This language-family has two broad divisions, namely, Austroasiatic and Austronesian. The Austroasiatic languages are spoken by some populations of India, Burma and Indo-China. For example, the Kols and Mundas of Central India, the Nicobarese of Nicobar islands and the Khasis of Meghalaya belong to this linguistic group. The Austronesian division includes three sub-divisions like Indonesian, Melanesian and Polynesian.

Culture

The Australoids were primarily hunters and gatherers, though they had the knowledge of primitive agriculture. Digging stick was their principal implement with the help of which they collected roots and tubers as well as practised primitive farming. At a later stage in some parts of India they carried on terrace cultivation, a method widely practised in southeast Asia. Probably they were the people to tame elephant for the first time in India. They had their settlements mostly in the hill slopes and forests.

They acquired the art of making earthen pot. But perhaps they had no knowledge of using wheel for that purpose. They shaped pottery with the help of hand. Sarkar suggested that perhaps "their technique of pot making was by scooping the earth out of solid mass of clay in order to give it shape of a pot or by putting strips of clay on the inner side of the basket and then burning it in fire". Boomerang, which is still in use among the Irulas of Madras forest, was perhaps widely used by the Australoid to kill small games and birds. The present day Australian aborigines also use this implement. It appears that the Australoids did not know the use of bow and arrow.

The religious practices of the Australoids centred round animism and ancestral worship. Each clan drew the line of descent from an eponymous ancestor in the form of an animal, tree or such other natural objects. It is believed that the totemic belief is the main contribution of the Australoids. The shaman or medicine-man played a very vital role in the Australoid society. The initiation ceremony is another important aspect of their social life. During this ceremony the teeth of the young were chipped or filed. The same practice is still in vague among the Kadars of Kerala. Another trait is circumcision of the boys. This is, however, no longer practised by the Australoid tribes of India, but it is very much present among the Australian aborigines, the true representative of the Australoids.

It must be admitted that the present day Australoids of India are so mixed culturally and ethnically with other populations groups that it is not at all easy to isolate the original form of the Australoids, more particularly in the cultural field. Even then a minute and careful scrutiny of the physical features and cultural traits of the mixed people of India bring to light some Australoid elements in them.

Origin and Migration

The opinion as regards the origin and migration of the Australoids expressed by various competent authorities differ. According to Sarkar (1954) "The ancestors of the Australoids came from eastern Mediterranean area. Early branches of them passed through India into Southeast Asia and Australia. South India as centre, the Australoids fanned out both to east and west, and they appear at one time to have been more widespread. They were pushed by later immigrants to different regions to form isolated groups". A similar view was expressed by Hutton (1931) also. He wrote "The Protoaustraloids ... whose origin must be sought in Palestine, where up to the present, the earliest ancestors of their race have been found, may claim to be the true aborigines on the ground that their racial type was ultimately fixed in India". Chatterjee (1951) is also of the opinion that "The next people to come to India... would appear to be the Proto-Australoid — a medium dolichocephalic race from the Eastern Mediterranean."

Again, there is a possibility that some entered

India from the east also. One can perhaps think of two possible routes of migration from the east, one via north Myanmar and then through Arunachal Pradesh, and the other is through the Imphal valley. In India at one time they appear to have spread over the entire country, but now they are in some sort of isolated pockets because as has already been mentioned they were pushed into different regions by the newcomers.

Khasi

In this context the Khasis who mainly live in Meghalaya deserve a special treatment, because though they are Mongoloid, they speak Austric language which is somehow associated with the Australoids. The Austric speaking Khasis are surrounded by various tribes belonging to the Tibeto-Burman linguistic group. Thus, linguistically the Khasis are a very distinct populations forming an isolated pocket among the Tibeto-Burman tribes. Ethnically, however, all these populationss are members of the Indo-Mongoloid. Dixon wrote that "the Khasis in spite of their linguistic isolation among the people of Assam, are racially closely related to the majority of the Tibeto-Burman tribes. With them they represent a very old western drift of southwestern Asia peoples. Unlike their neighbours, however, they have succeeded in retaining their old speech". Hutton is also of opinion that the Khasis, though, have managed to maintain their Austric language, differ little in physique from the Tibeto-Burman speaking peoples. The present writer (1970, 1978) studied the physical characteristics of the Khasis in details, compared them with other tribal populations groups of northeast India and found that "instead of affiliating the Khasis to any of these groups, it can, in general be said that all the groups are short to medium in height. All are characterised by mesocephalic head, mesorrhine nose and low and broad face."

Chatterjee has very clearly explained this situation. Therefore, it is supposed to be better to quote him : "They would appear to be a Mongoloid people who have adopted the language of the earlier race, the Austrics (or Proto-Australoid), after they have come down south from the Tibeto-Burman area of dispersion. They may have changed their speech to the Austric (Mon-Khmer) Khasi even while they were in Burma : and after that they may have come to Assam and ensconced themselves in the Khasi and Jaintia Hills successfully resisting all possible attempts of the Bodos who followed them in dislodging or absorbing them. It is equally likely that they were a congeries of diverse Tibeto-Burman speaking tribes in the Khasi and Jaintia Hills and in the plains of Sylhet, settling among the original Austric speakers, whose language the Tibeto-Burman settlers in this area found convenient to adopt when their own tribal dialects were too numerous and too diverse. Possibly this linguistic change-over occurred before the coming of the waves of Bodo expansion".

All these facts suggest two possibilities regarding the origin and affiliation of the Khasis. One is that they were racially Mongoloid but have adopted the Austric language. The other possibility is that the Khasis were an Australoid people and their language was Austric. In course of time their physical features were modified by Mongoloid strains. Their physical features have undergone remarkable changes, but their language has been retained.

The Khasis are matriarchal people. In a family authority is vested on the mother; property is inherited by the daughters; descent is matrilineal and after marriage a girl does not go to live in the house of the husband.

In general, it can be said that the Khasis have brown skin colour. Their head hair is dark brown with a reddish tinge in colour, straight on flat, wavy in form and coarse in texture. They have scantly beard and moustache. The colour of eye is brown to dark brown. The eye slit is mostly oblique and palpebral fissure is medium. Eye fold is present in most of the cases. They are short in stature. Their head is mesocephalic and nose is mesorrhine.

In this context it may perhaps be mentioned that the Wanchoos of Arunachal use some Austric words in their dialect. The presence of certain Australoid racial elements also become discernible in their physical features, when they are minutely observed with trained eyes. At the present state of knowledge it is difficult to offer an explanation of the situation. But one can perhaps speculate the possibility of the Austric speakers passing through the present day habitat of the Wanchoos leaving behind certain racial and cultural elements in the region.

Though the root of the Assamese language is Sanskrit, when it passed through different stages to acquire its present form, it incorporated in it several Austric words. Therefore, it is quite likely that Australoid racial elements as well as Austric words have entered into the Caucasoid Assamese populations and the Assamese language respectively.

Mongoloid Element in Assam

It has already been mentioned that in the ancient Sanskrit literature we come across a populations called the Kiratas who were non-Aryan. They were occupying the different regions in the Himalayas and the northeastern region of India. The Kiratas were Mongoloid people. They include the Cinas (or the Chinese), the Bhotas (or the Tibetans) and other Mongoloid populationss. As has already been stated the Aryans were quite aware of the fact that the yellowish-skinned Mongoloid Kiratas were very much different from the dark-skinned Nishada, the Australoid autocthones of India, and therefore, they used two different terms to denote the two different non-Aryan peoples.

Kirata

For the first time the mention of the term Kirata has been found in the *Yajurveda* (XXX. 16). It is written that for the performance of Purushamedha sacrifice, along with other articles, a Kirata is necessary: "A Kirata for the caves a Jambhaka for the slopes; a Kimpurusha for the mountains" (translated by S.K. Chatterjee). In the *Atharvaveda* (X.4-14) also, we find mention of the Kirata : "The young maid of Kirata race, a little damsel, digs the drug. Digs it with shovels wrought of gold on the high ridges of the hills" (translated by Chatterjee). Thus, these suggest that the Kiratas lived in caves. How far it is true, it is difficult to ascertain, but it is quite likely that their habitat was in the hills and forests. The girl was digging soil on the high ridges of the hills, which indicates that perhaps they were food gatherers and that they had some knowledge of herbal medicine. At present also, they practise all these traits. The Vedas are supposed to have been complied around tenth century B.C. Therefore, the mention of the

Kiratas in the Vedas implies that at least at that time, if not earlier they were distributed in the slopes of the Himalayas and other regions in the north and northeast.

That the Kiratas were dependant on collection of fruits, roots and tubers is evident form the references found in the *Mahabharata*. In the Sabhaparvan of the *Mahabharata*, there is mention of Nakul's meeting the Kiratas on his march towards northwest. Those "Kiratas were living on fruits and roots, clad in skins, fierce with their weapons, cruel in their deeds." Then again in the *Mahabharata*, Bhim on his eastward journey, after crossing the Videha country met the Kiratas : "Then the Pandava hero, O son of Kunti, coming to the Videha land close to Indra Mountain, defeated the seven Kirata rulers" (translated by Chatterjee). This suggests that the Kiratas were dominating in the east. Further, in the Kirataparvan, a section of the Vanaparvan of the *Mahabharata*, we find references to the Kiratas. There is a clear indication that the Kiratas were yellow (gold like) in skin colour.

In the Periplus of the Erythroean Sea, a Greek work of the first century A.D., we find mention of a populations called the Kirrhadee described as "race of men with flattened nose". They lived in the hills of Assam and Burma. They are no others than the Kiratas. The same work suggests that their territory was extended as far as Bengal and Orissa.

In a very ancient time there was a king, called Mahiranga Danava, in Kamarupa or Pragjyotisha. The word danava suggests that he was a non-Aryan king. It is said that the king derived his name from a hillock named Mairang, near modern Guwahati. Mahiranga is a Sanskritized form of Mairang. The root of this term can be traced from a Boro word. This king was a Kirata and his subjects were also Kiratas. After Mahiranga, Hatakasur ascended the throne. He was followed by Sambarasur respectively. They were Kirata kings ruling over the Kirata subjects.

In the writings of the late medieval period also the Mongoloid inhabitants of eastern India have been referred to as the Kiratas. For instance, in the Rajamala chronicle of the Tripura kings (16th century A.D.) and in the Yoginitantra (post 16th century) we come across the term Kirata.

Thus, in the languages of Chatterjee, it may be summarised that the "Kiratas were known to the Hindu world as a group of peoples whose original home was in the Himalayan slopes and in the mountains of the east, in Assam particularly, who were yellow in colour and presented a distinct type of culture. They had spread all over the plains of Bengal upto the sea". They preferred to live in the hills and forests. They collected forest products and minerals. They were expert weavers. They kept contact with neighbouring peoples through trade. These Kiratas are the Indo-Mongoloids of the present time.

It is an established fact that all the tribes of north-east India are basically Mongoloid. They came to this part of the country in successive waves at different times from different routes—north, northeast and southeast. Some groups became confined to certain small geographical areas, while others were distributed over larger regions. Some of them were more or less in complete isolation preserving their ethno-biological identity, while some had got admixtured with non-Mongoloid populations to varying extents. The Mongoloid tribes of India are referred to as the Indo-Mongoloids.

Physical Feature

In general the physical features of the Mongoloids can be described as follows : Yellow or yellowish-brown skin colour. Black, stretched or flat wavy and coarse head hair. Scanty growth of facial and body hair. Black or dark brown eye colour; oblique slit and narrow palpebral fissure; brown face with prominent zygomatic arches. One of the typical characteristics of the Mongoloids is the presence of Mongolian fold in their eyes.

Many of the Indo-Mongoloids of north India,

more particularly of Assam, however, do not show marked or typical Mongoloid traits in their physical features. In Assam Haddon identified one type called the Brachycephalic-platyrrhine type, which according to him is a variety of the Pareoean. The Pareoeans are known as Southern Mongoloid also. Haddon observed that, "most of the people of this group became considerably mixed with the local non-Mongolian races when they came south". Moreover, Haddon believed in the occurrence of a strong Nesiot element (dolichocephalic-mesorrhine) among the Nagas and other hill tribes to which reference has already been made earlier. However, he found it difficult to isolate the Nesiot type as it was almost everywhere mixed with a brachycephalic xanthoderm (yellow-skinned) stock. As has already been mentioned, in Assam the Mongoloids in the very early time intermixed with the Australoids also. Asides, they came in contact with the different types of the Caucasoids. From each of them entered certain genes to the Indo-Mongoloids of Assam and as a result they acquired varied physical types to be distinctiveness of the different groups.

Assam Tribe and Asiatic Mongoloid

In 1970 the present writer made a comparison of the Assam tribes with some of the Mongoloid populationss of Asia in respect of stature, head, face and nose. For this purpose, the numerically large and at the same time representative populationss were taken into account. The data were taken from the tables prepared by Buchi in 1965. Here I propose to quote what was found : "The mean values of stature of the various populationss under consideration reveal that most of the people are medium statured. A short statured element is encountered among the Mois and the Samre of Indo-China, the Lepcha of Sikkim, the Newar and the Khambu of Nepal and some of the northeast Indian tribes like Kuki, Khasi and Abor. The means of the Boro, Naga, Khamyang of northeast India and that of the Pa Miao and the Thais of Yunnan lie on the borderline between short and medium. Thus, in respect of stature the Assam tribes are well within the Mongoloid populations of Asia. They show more resemblance to the people of South-China and Indo-China, the Moi and the Lao of Siam, the Gurkha, the Limbu, the Newar and the Khambu of Nepal, the Lepcha and the Bhotia than to the other people. The people of Tibet, Turkestan and Mongolia are comparatively much taller than the tribes of Assam. It is significant that in most of the regions, the stature decreases from the north to the south.

Almost all the populations have brachycephalic heads, except the people of Tibet, Mois of Annam, Newar of Nepal, Lepcha and Bhotia, but they also show a tendency towards brachycephaly in the sense that they have high mesocephalic heads. This tendency is seen in the Deori and Mishing of Assam. Otherwise, the Assam tribes differ from the other populationss in having mesocephalic heads. The differences are more due to the breadth of the head than to the length. The Assam tribes have narrower heads than the others.

The people of Tibet have much longer and broader heads than the Assam tribes; the same is true as regards the people of Mongolia. The Chinese, Koreans, the peoples of Indo-China and Siam, on the other hand, differ from the Assam tribes in having much broader heads.

In general, the Assam tribes have narrower faces than the other people, and in this way they differ from the others. In respect of total facial index, (length of face in relation to its breadth) they show some sort of similarities with the peoples of Indo-China and Siam.

Although most of the populations are characterized by a mesorrhine nose, differences are observed among the mean values. In general, the Assam tribes have broader noses than most of the other peoples. In some populations of Mongolia, Korea, China, Nepal, Indo-China and Siam, noses broader than those of the Assam tribes are also observed.

The above comparison reveals that the Assam tribes show some similarities in one or other characters with the Mongoloid populationss of Asia, but they have certain individuality. In general, it can be said that they are shorter, they have narrow heads, narrower faces and broader noses in comparison to the other Asiatic Mongoloids."

The present writer (1970) compared the tribes of northeast India with some Mongoloid populationss of Asia in respect of percentile occurrence of ABO blood group genes also. As in case of anthropometry in case of blood groups also, numerically large and representative populationss were taken into consideration. They are : Chinese, Burmese, Japanese, Tibetans, Javanese, Nepal-Sikim-Bhutan, Siamese, Thai, Lao, Moi, Khmer, Nicobarese and Vietnamese.

The Mongoloid people of southeast Asia occupy a distinct position among the others. So do the Japanese and the Chinese. The tribes of northeast India are very close to the people of Nepal, Sikkim and Bhutan, but they have a position between the Japanese and the Chinese. It is to be noted that they are very similar to the people of southeast Asia and thus they occupy a place in the complex of southeast Asia in respect of percentile distribution of ABO blood group genes.

The frequency of the gene A decreases from

the north to the south. The highest frequency of this gene is seen in the Japanese and the lowest in the peoples of southeast Asia. In between these two extremes, stand the peoples of Nepal, Sikkim and Bhutan, the tribes of northeast India and the Chinese. On the other hand the frequency of B gene increases as one proceeds from the north to the south. The Nicobarese, another Mongoloid population, stand far apart from the other Asiatic Mongoloids. This may, perhaps be a case of genetic drift followed by isolation.

Taste ability to a chemical substance called phenylthiocarbomide (PTC) is also considered to be a genetic marker and is taken into account for studying affiliations among populations. Among the Assam tribes the frequency of persons who are unable to taste this substance (non-taster) ranges between 7 to 22 per cent. This is well within the range of the Mongoloids.

Mongoloid Tribal Groups

According to the present writer (1970) the Mongoloid tribes of northeast India may conveniently be grouped under the (i) Khasi; (ii) Boro; (iii) Lushai-Kuki; (iv) Naga; (v) Arunachal tribes and (vi) 'Others'. The basis of this grouping is one or the other factors like (a) linguistic affinity; (b) cultural similarity; (c) common territory ; and (d) biological closeness.

In the present context of the people of Assam, the Arunachal tribes do not deserve much consideration. The Khasis are met with in the southern border of Middle Assam, while the Nagas mostly inhabit the adjoining territories of Nagaland, their home state. The representatives of the Lushai-Kuki are distributed in the southern border, mostly of the central region. The 'Others' tribes are distributed in different parts of the State. This category includes besides certain tribes, for example, Mishing, Deori, etc. The 'Boro' forms one of the most important tribal groups of Assam.

It has been stated that various tribal groups like the Boro, Naga, Karbi, Kuki-Chin speak Tibeto-Burman languages. The term Boro is used in different senses. There is a tribe called the Boro, Boro Kachari, Again, under the Boro linguistic group the Garo, Kachari, Rabha, Mech, Tiwa, etc., are also very often listed. Sometimes it is used in racial sense also.

Tibeto-Burman Migration

The original homeland of the speakers of the Tibeto-Burman languages is considered to be the upper courses of the Yangtse Kiang and the Hoang-ho rivers in southwest China. At one time a group of the Tibeto-Burman people left their original habitat and migrated towards south. Somewhere in north-eastern Burma the group split up. One group moved towards further south to reach as far as southeast Asia, while one group migrated westward following the foot-hills of the Himalayas and reached as far as Nepal, Tibet and Bhutan, and at a later date in successive waves, from there they migrated to the south to occupy the valleys and hills of Assam. S.K. Chatterjee suggests "It seems quite probable that long before 1000 B.C., some of these early Tibeto-Burmans had penetrated within the frontiers of India, either along the southern slopes of the Himalayas, or by way of Tibet". On their way to southeast Asia some members of the first group changed their direction and moved westwards to enter into different parts of northeast India. All these populationss scattered themselves in different parts of northeast India and came to be known by various names like the Boro, Naga, Kuki, Tiwa, etc. The third group entered Assam by the Brahmaputra valley. Thus, it appears that the various Indo-Mongoloid populationss now known by different names came to Assam by various routes and at different times.

There is no historical records to tell us as regards the origin and migration of the Tibeto-Burman tribes. But certain legends prevalent among some of the Boro tribes help us to trace the route of migration of the respective tribes. For instance, Playfair (1909) in his monograph on the Garos elaborately dealt with the migratory routes of the Garos. Their ancestral home was Tibet from where they came down to occupy their present habitat, the Garo hills and the adjoining areas. Instead of going into details giving by Playfair, the outline of this traditional story can briefly be presented in the following manner.

Garo : The ancestors of the Garos inhabited in Toura, a province in Tibet, from where under the leadership of two chiefs they moved southward to arrive at Rangamati, a locality in the plains region of the northern part of the Goalpara district in Assam. From there they moved further south to reach Dhubri, a district headquarter. The then local king of that region was quite friendly with the immigrants, but the former did not like the idea to permit the latter to settle permanently in his kingdom. As a result they had to move eastward following the northern bank of the Brahmaputra to reach its affluent Manas river. There they had to fight against a local chief, who defeated them. After that near Jogighopa, they crossed the Brahmaputra and arrived at the south bank of the river, that is, South Goalpara. Somewhere there, a local chief named Arambit married a girl of the immigrant group, that is, the progenitors of the Garos. Arambit permitted the immigrants to establish their settlement on Baghmela Pahar, a hill near Boko, a small township of modern time. From there again on different occasions they spread in different directions, and finally they formed different groups inhabiting different areas. This populations group was the ancestors of the modern day Garo.

Playfair did not ignore certain cultural elements in the Garos to suggest that these elements "owe their origin to the land from which they claim to have come". For example, an animal called yak, which has never been seen by the modern Garos, plays a notable role in the tradition of the Garo. Yak's tail has an important place in their socio-cultural life. The gongs, which are of Tibetan origin, are proud possessions of the Garos and use them on some specific occasions.

Rabha : The present writer collected one such traditional story prevalent among the Rabhas, an examination of which gives some idea about their route of migration. The story was published elsewhere (1960), which is reproduced here :

In the remote past, there was a very powerful king, whose name was Dadan. His father's name was Haha (or Kalpuk), and Huhu (or Michi) was mother. He married a girl, called Toba Rani.

Originally he was at Sonitpur (modern Tezpur). At that time he was not a king, but the leader of a group of people. Ban, the mythological Hindu king, ruled that country and Dadan was somehow related to him. However, their exact relationship is not well-known. Probably Dadan was a general of the then sovereign king, Ban.

After the death of Ban, Dadan had to fight with

some other peoples of the east and of the south of Sonitpur. He won the first battle, but being defeated in the second had to leave that place with some of his followers and proceed to Bhutan in search of aid and shelter. The king of Bhutan, however, refused.

Dadan accompanied by his wife, sister Sosho, sister's daughter Jhano, Jhano's husband Maru Khetri (who was a Kshatriya by caste) and his followers moved from Bhutan towards the Brahmaputra valley via Doangiri, that is, through modern Kamrup, and arrived at Bakbua hill near Barpeta. There they rested for a short period, then proceeding along the bank of river Chaulkhowa entered Goalpara district. Near Jogighopa they crossed the Brahmaputra and reached Pancharatna near which there was a beel called Hachila. The party spent a brief period there and after that they moved southwards following the course of a rivulet, named Duldunga and ultimately reached Dubu hill near modern Lakhipur.

Dadan first established his kingdom in that area. He made Maru Khetri his general and gradually tried to bring the surrounding areas under his rule. His fort was at Tikirkilla, where he stationed the major portion of his force. In nearby Nokornong forest he trained his soldiers. It is said that even now ruins of the thrones, where king Dadan and his wife Toba Rani took their seats and watched the trainings of the soldiers are there.

He kept his soldiers in small groups in different places, and accordingly each group took its clan name after some important object of respective locality—it might be a hillock, a stream and so forth. Dadan was a very brave warrior and he had to resist the aggression of various kings, such as, Khasi Raja, Brek, Mermer, Murmur, Chamtrong. And in every battle Maru Khetri was his right hand man. The seventh battle was fought between Dadan on one side, and Arimatta, Brichand and Chikrong on the other. Maru Khetri was killed in that battle and Dadan lost the battle.

Dadan accompanied by his wife, sister, sister's daughter fled to Tura, from where they moved to Darmarh hill and settled there. Dadan had a mind to organise a new force. For that purpose he had to roam about in that area, unfortunately, without having any weapon with him. In the mean time Arimatta sent some of his soldiers in disguise to find out Dadan. One day two of them met Dadan and attacked him, Dadan uprooted a tree and killed them. At that moment a third soldier came and from a distance released an arrow which penetrated the body of Dadan. Dadan fell down and died.

The descendants of Dadan and his followers

are the Rabha of South Goalpara of the present day.

It should be borne in mind that since long past the legends have been passed orally from generation to generation and hence, there may have been many changes in the names of the places as well as persons. The circumstances under which a group had to move may not also give the same picture. For example, the story of the Rabha migration is told with some minor variations by different persons inhabiting different regions. According to some, Dadan's wife's name was Nodai. Toba Rani was the daughter of his sister Jhimari. Again, to other Toba Rani was the niece of Dadan. Her daughter was Nodai who was married to Maru Khetri. Whatever that might be, the legends give some idea about the migration of the different populations groups and also their encounter with other people.

There are some other legends also prevalent among these populationss. According to one such story the Rangdani Rabhas, a section of the Rabha tribe lived in the Garo Hills alongwith the Garos. Very often the two tribes came into conflict with one another. Therefore, finally the Rangdani Rabhas had to leave their hilly habitat and came down to settle in the plains. Another story narrates that the Rangdani Rabhas and the Atongs, a section of the Garos, are descendants of two sisters called Sae-Bonge and Bonge-Kate respectively. Playfair has pointed out to linguistic similarities between the Rangdani Rabhas and the Atongs, asides some other cultural traits.

Kachari : Thus, the traditional stories told by the Rabhas and the Garos suggest that Tibet or eastern sub-Himalayan region was their ancestral home, from where they migrated to Assam. They did not follow the same route. Moreover, at that time they were not known by their respective present names. The people from these regions came to northeast India not in one migration but in successive times. One such migration brought the Kacharis. Endle (1911) believes that the original homeland of the Kacharis also was Tibet and China. According to him there were at least two great migrations of the Kacharis. One wave came from the north. They entered western Assam through the valley of Tista, Sonkosh and founded their kingdom in that area. The other migration was from the northeast (the third group mentioned earlier). They made their way through the Subansiri, Dibong and Dihing valley in Assam. According to some, the Chutiyas and Morans also perhaps came by this route. Both were very old Mongoloid peoples of Assam. The Morans had their own kingdom till the arrival of the Ahoms, who defeated the former and established their own kingdom. In Upper Assam the Chutiyas too, had their own kingdom, which flourished for a long time. Thus, some scholars believe that originally they were akin to the Boro people.

Taking the Brahmaputra river as the dividing line, Endle has divided the Boro populations into two major groups, namely, southern and northern according to their distribution. The legends prevalent among the Rabhas and Garos indicate that they crossed the Brahmaputra to reach the south bank. The habitat of the Garos is on the south bank. The Dimasa moved further south to settle in the North Cachar Hills. Another group migrated further southwest to arrive at Tripura and the adjoining areas, where they are referred to as the Hill Tripura. The Tiwas live in the south bank of Middle Assam. However, not all the populationss crossed the Brahmaputra to settle in the south bank. Many members of them were left behind in the north bank and now they are occupying different regions in the north of the Brahmaputra. Again, the Boros may be divided into the western group and the eastern group. The Rabha, Mech, Garo are some of the members of the western group, while the Sonowal, Thengal, Jharua, etc., belong to the eastern group.

There are many similarities between the Garos and the Kacharis, and therefore, Playfair thinks that "the two tribes were originally one and the same". In support of his view he has pointed out to the possible way of their bifurcation, their distribution in different regions, language and so forth. A Garo legend suggests that the Kacharis are the descendants of a Garo girl, who married a non-Garo boy, when the ancestors of the Garos lived in Jogighopa.

Karbi **:** Another such wave of migration brought the ancestors of the Karbis (Mikir) who are now concentrated in the Karbi Anglong district of Assam. They form an interesting tribe in the sense that though they speak Tibeto-Burman language, they are neither put under the Boro nor any other linguistic group. They show some sort of linguistic affinities with many of the tribes. According to some the Karbi language has some similarities with the Naga dialects on one hand and Lushai - Kuki on the other. Grierson (1904) put them in an intermediate position between the Boro and the western Naga on the basis of language. Some authorities are of the opinion that the Karbi language shows a mixture of Austric and Boro language though it is certain that they belong to Tibeto-Burman linguistic family. Lyall (1881), however, long back said that the Karbis are more similar to the Boro than to the Khasi.

The Karbis also tell about their traditional stories of migration. But most of the stories refer to their migration in and around their present habitat. Examining these stories, in general, it can be said that perhaps they first made their settlement in the eastern region of the Khasi and Jaintia Hills. But for some reasons they could not go along well with the latter. Therefore, they moved to the Kachari kingdom and reached Dimapur. There too, they could not live in amity with the Kacharis for a longer time. They had to move again. Thus, the stories suggest that the Karbis being surrounded by the Khasi, Kachari and Naga were pushed from one place to another within a limited territory at different times before finally settling in Karbi Anglong. Therefore, they came in contact with different tribal groups from whom they picked up certain cultural elements including language.

Ahom : In the historical period Assam witnessed a very significant wave of Mongoloid migration which brought the Ahoms. They came from Upper Burma by the northeastern route crossing the Patkoi ranges in the early part of the thirteenth century. They form a member of the Thai or Shan group, and unlike the Tibeto-Burman populations of Assam, linguistically they belong to the Siamese-Chinese branch of the Sino-Tibetan language family. The Ahoms first established their kingdom in Upper Assam, and then they extended their territory down the Brahmaputra valley. Though the Ahoms were originally Thai or Shan speakers, coming to Assam they gradually abandoned their language and accepted Assamese language. By the sixteenth and seventeenth centuries they became Hindu.

At later dates the Ahoms were followed by some other Shan groups, for example, Khamti, Tai Phake, Aiton, Turung, Khamyang, etc. They too, came from the same direction. Each of them forms a small populations group and has their settlement in particular pockets in Upper Assam.

In this connection it should be recalled that the purpose of the present discussion is not to describe the migration of the different tribes of Assam. A few have been cited as example in order to show the entry of the Mongoloid people from different directions and in different times, and also to give indication how each one settled in different parts and assumed different names. Another point is to be noted that the Mongoloid migration to Assam was started in an undateable past and continued till recent period.

Keith's View

The eminent physical anthropologist Sir Arthur Keith (1936) once drew the attention of the anthropologists to that fact that there is a possibility of evolution of certain racial types in India itself. He wrote : "At least it is urgently necessary that our eyes should be more directly focussed on the probability of India being an evolutionary field—both now and in former times." Why is it that "her part in the past has been to receive and not to give?" He observed that the type represented by the Telegu Brahmins which Guha regarded as the essential and prevalent Indian type, might have evolved from the Veddid (Australoid) type. Sarkar fully agreed with this view of Keith. With the help of scientific data and proper examples and sound arguments, he has discussed in details the probable mode of evolution and has come to the conclusion that "the present day Dravidians have evolved from the Veddid (Australoid) type through changes caused in their physical features by the varied environmental conditions". Unfortunately, Sarkar's view has not widely been circulated and the scholars have not given due consideration and thought on this subject. We have sufficient examples to establish that in certain parts of the globe, different ethnic groups have emerged from the ancestral stock by way of microevolutionary trends. Anyway, though there are reasons to believe that there is a great possibility of the Dravidian type evolving from an earlier stock in India, yet here let us bring the Dravidians from outside India.

Caucasoid Element in Assam

The Caucasoid is a major racial group of mankind, which includes several types and sub-types. The Mediterranean is a variety of the Caucasoid. In general the Mediterraneans have wavy or even curly black hair. They are medium-statured people and are of slender build. They are dolichocephalic people having narrow oval face and low orbits. Their forehead is vertical with protruding occiput. Their nose is mesorrhine, though leptorrhine noses are also met with. The eyes are generally very dark. The Mediterranean type also has several varieties and they exhibit minor variations among themselves in respect of physical features.

Mediterranean

After the Australoids different varieties of the Mediterranean types came to India in successive waves. The earliest one was dolichocephalic people of the Palaeo-Mediterranean stock, which was closely related to the Proto-Mediterranean or Proto - Egyptian Brown Race. The physical features of the Brown Race has been described by Elliot Smith as follows: long head; small stature; scanty hair on body and face; body of slender build; eyebrows poorly developed or absent; bulged-out occiput; forehead narrow, vertical or slightly bugging; face short, narrow, and usually orthognathous, etc. They were widely distributed over a very large area including both the shores of Mediterranean, peninsula of Arabia, South Persia, Mesopotamia, Syria, coastal part of Asia Minor, etc. Therefore, as regards this Brown Race Elliot Smith says that "it is clear that we cannot call this group 'Hamitic', because it includes such

Semites as the Arabs; nor can we call it 'Mediterranean', for its domain has been extended far beyond the limits of the Middle Sea, and also its distribution is not that assigned by Sergi to the Mediterranean Race." The later waves of migration brought to India the more basic type of the Mediterranean races.

At one time the Mediterranean people formed an unbroken chain extending from eastern Mediterranean through India to southeast Asia. These Mediterranean people include the Brown Race of Elliot Smith also. At later dates movements of different peoples started, many new types emerged and as a result this chain was broken into pieces dispersing the people into isolated pockets. In some cases the admixture between the earlier settlers and the new comers was of such extent that the former completely lost their original ethnic and cultural identity. We have already mentioned that Haddon noticed one such element among the Nagas. This type which is characterized by dolichocephalic head and mesorrhine nose is called the Nesiot or Indonesian. The presence, of such traits among the Indo-Mongoloids of northeast India contributed by the ancient Mediterraneans gives an indication that at very ancient time certain type of Mediterranean people migrated to Assam.

An analysis of the prehistoric and proto-historic

human remains suggests that from the very ancient time different ethnic elements entered into the populations of India. For example, the skeletal remains of the Indus Valley yielded four different types. One type is comparable to the Proto-Nordic. One type is undoubtedly Palaeo-Mediterranean or Mediterranean, while another type is Australoid. Again, the fourth type is Alpine-Armenoid, which is marked by brachycephaly. Others are dolichocephalic people.

The Mohenjodaro crania have been divided into four groups according to their racial affinity by Sewell and Guha. Three crania are Australoid, six are of Mediterranean type, one is Mongoloid and four are probably Alpinoid. According to B.K. Chatterjee and G.D. Kumar (1963) the Harappa collection comprised of four racial types and these are : Proto-Nordic, Proto-Mediterranean, Alpino-Armenoid and Australoid. Therefore, though it is said that the Indus Valley civilization is a contribution of the Mediterranean people, we find in Indus Valley people of different ethnic stocks.

While discussing the position of the Asiatic Proto-Mediterranean, Cappieri (1961) observed that the ancient people of the area between Agean and the indus valley were originally long headed. They remain substantially the same for a long period. The brachycephalic element akin to the Alpine or Armenoid appears to be later immigrant.

Probably they came from northeast of Asia Minor, Iranian and Pamir plateau. Sewell and Guha also bring the Alpine-Armenoid element from west. Dixon thinks that during the period of third to second millennium B.C. a Palaeo-Alpine element entered India through the northwestern route. Whatever that might be, it could perhaps be said that the dolichocephalic Proto-Mediterranean or Mediterranean people came to India from the west. The brachycephalic Alpine-Armenoid people followed the Mediterranean or came almost at the same time from the west or northwest. Prior to the migration of these people, India was inhabited by the Australoids.

A type of Mediterranean people is considered to be the builders of the Indus Valley civilization. They were not only confined to the north. That at one time the Mediterranean people were distributed over a large area of India is evident from the skeletal and other materials collected from different regions of India including south India. The remains bring to the light their antiquity also. The Indo-Dravidians are Mediterranean people. However, with the coming of the Indo-Aryans, the Indo-Dravidians started loosing their hold in the northern part of the country.

It is not perfectly known at what time the Mediterranean people, a variety of the Caucasoid race entered Assam. We have already referred to the Brown Race and existence of Nesiot element in certain populations, a suggestive of Mediterranean migration into this part of the country in a very ancient time. However, it is difficult to ascertain the time.

Narakasur defeated Ghatakasur, the Kirata ruler of Pragjyotisha and ascended the throne. The term Asur means that Narakasur was non-Aryan. He was brought up by the king of Videha, with the help of whom at a later date he defeated the Kiratas. After ascending the throne Narakasur married Maya, daughter of the king of Videha. The Videha king was Indo - Dravidian or Mediterranean. His subjects, if not all, at least a part, were also of the same race. Narakasur himself might also belong to the Mediterranean type. Thus, there is a possibility of flow of the Mediterranean people to Assam during that period. Again, according to K.L. Barua (1936), Pragjyotish itself was a Mediterranean kingdom. The Indo-Mongoloids, coming from the northeast occupied the territory and ruled over it. Narakasur, with the help of the king of Videha freed the country from the hands of the Indo-Mongoloids. If that is so, the Mediterranean type existed before the coming of Narakasur. This may be an old wave of the Mediterranean invasion.

It is an established fact that because of varied environmental conditions and for certain biological reasons, variation in respect of physical features (also in socio-cultural aspects) among the various populations of the same ethnic origin becomes apparent. In south India the Mediterranean developed into the Indo-Dravidian type. In northeast India the Mediterranean type may have acquired physical features different from that of the Indo-Dravidians. Therefore, instead of using the term Indo-Dravidian let us use the word Mediterranean at the moment to refer to the original type. Mediterranean element is very much noticeable in the present day populations of Assam. But on account of environmental factor and admixture, the Mediterranean type of Assam has assumed a different shape.

Alpine-Armenoid

We have already noted Alpine-Armenoid element alongwith the Mediterraneans and others in the populations of prehistoric and proto-historic India. The Mediterraneans are dolichocephalic, while the Alpines are characterized by brachycephaly. The Iranian plateau of Asia Minor and the Pamirian region are considered to be the original homeland of the Alpines. They entered India from the northwestern direction. Some are of opinion that the Alpine-Armenoid element entered Assam via the foot-hills of the Himalayas. According to K.L. Barua prior to the advent of the Vedic Aryans, the Alpines made notable contribution to the growth and development of the culture and civilization of eastern India. But subsequently superimposition of the Vedic Aryan traits made the earlier Alpine traits indistinct. He examined the Alpine elements of Assam from different angles—cultural, linguistic, historical and anthropological. He is of opinion that certain cultural traits connected with disposal of dead, uncleanliness of a woman during menses, etc., as found among the Assamese Hindus have their roots in the Alpine culture. He had analysed the linguistic aspect also. According to Barua there is little doubt that the Assamese Brahmins, Kayasthas and Kalitas were originally Alpine people. He has described the Alpines as brachycephalic people with leptorrhine nose. During his time there was not sufficient anthropometric data on these castes to put forward in support of his view, he said. He was, however, hopeful that an anthropometric survey on these castes was likely to prove his hypothesis. But such an anthropometric survey carried out by us (Das *et al* 1985-86) showed that among the present day Assamese people, these types of Alpine characteristics were insignificant. For example, approximately 56 per cent of the Brahmins are mesocephalic, and only about 34 per cent are brachycephalic. In average they are mesocephalic. The nasal index is also on the border line between leptorrhine and mesorrhine. However, about 59 per cent of them have leptorrhine nose. About 57 per cent of them are medium statured, with a tendency towards short. As regards the Kalitas, our study revealed that they are also medium in stature (about 62 per cent). About 50 per cent of them are mesocephalic and about 28 per cent are brachycephalic, the mean cephalic index being mesocephalic. Again 52 per cent and 44 per cent of them are mesorrhine and leptorrhine respectively, the mean being mesorrhine.

The above facts bring to light that among the present day Assamese people Alpine-Armenoid elements do not appear to predominate, rather they are inconspicuous. The high caste Assamese are by and large mesocephalic people showing tendency towards mesorrhine nose. Several factors may be responsible for this situation. One cannot ignore the biological factors, which are playing their respective roles. Again, perhaps the true Alpine variety did not reach Assam, only a few people of Alpine origin and that too, not in truly representative form entered Assam. According to K.L. Barua "the Maithil and Kanaujia Brahmins have proved to be hybrid type, either Mediterranean Alpine, or Mediterranean X Vedic Aryan." If it is so, hybridization of the Alpine either with the Mediterranean or with the Vedic Aryan already took place in Maithila or Kanauj, and this hybrid group migrated to Assam at a later date. Hence, the possibility of the entry of the true Alpine type to Assam is too remote. Again, in

Assam itself this mixed populations came in contact with the earlier immigrants, the dolichocephalic Mediterraneans. As a result, the characteristic Alpine traits became more indistinct. It must be admitted that many more possibilities may be speculated on account of lack of authentic information. But perhaps it is very true that the present day Assamese exhibit only faint traces of Alpinoid strains alongwith other varieties of Caucasoid physical features.

In this context mention may be made of the Kalitas of Assam, who according to some scholars are of Alpine origin, and they had early settlements (called Kalita desha) near about modern Sadiya. Their origin is still a subject of speculation in the absence of adequate and authentic information. P.C. Choudhury (1966) in his thesis has summarised the different views expressed by different authors as regards the position of the Kalitas. Therefore, I would prefer to quote him instead of going into further discussion. He wrote, "Kakati believed that there were early settlements of the Kalitas near Sadiya (Kalita desha). Neufvile locates the Kalitas in the same area and points to their ancient and high civilization. Dalton thinks that they were the earliest Aryan colonists of Assam, and were not Koch as held by Hodgson. Waddell thinks that they were of mixed descendants of the Indian Kayasthas. Robinson makes them spiritual guides of the Koch, whose, position is believed to have been degraded by the advent of the Brahmans; he supports Waddell's theory of the Kayastha origin of the Kalitas ... The common belief is that the Kalitas or their ancestors entered India from the west, settled in Upper India, and ultimately entered Assam, and that they were Kshatriyas. The Kshatriya origin is ascribed among others by Agarwal, Bordoloi and Bezbarua. In the opinion of Medhi, they were not Kshatriyas, but entered Assam before the Vedic Aryans and were non-Vedic Aryans." Choudhury believes that "in all appearance, the Kalitas stand for an ethnic types rather than a caste". What has been meant by 'an ethnic type' is, however, not very clearly defined. A comparison, of the physical characteristics of the Kalitas with those of some other Assamese castes does not disclose that the Kalitas significantly stand apart from the others. Again on the authority of Waddell, Choudhury writes that "Anthropometry also possibly indicates the Alpine origin of the Kalitas". He is perhaps not aware of the fact that Waddell's observation is not based on adequate anthropometric information. The Kalitas unlike the brachycephalic Alpines are, by and large mesocephalic people. Again, the Alpine nose is leptorrhine, whereas in average the Kalita nose is mesorrhine. Therefore, at the present state of our knowledge it will not be proper to say that the Kalitas represent an Alpine ethnic type.

Caucasoid from Northeast

It is generally believed that the Caucasoid elements entered India from the northwestern direction and gradually spread to Assam. But there are some scholars like Keane (1920) and others who have thought of the possibilities of entering Caucasoid element from northeastern direction as well. There are reasons to believe that at a very early time a group of Caucasoid people moved from the west through Mongolia and China to reach as far east as Japan. In course of time, expansion of the Mongoloids almost entirely eliminated this Caucasic strain. At present only a small Caucasoid populations, called the Ainu, is still surviving in Japan surrounded by Mongoloid people to give evidence of the said possibility of migration of the Caucasoids. Perhaps a small band of this Caucasoid people migrated southward and thereafter entered Assam via northeastern routes. It is not unlikely that the same routes were followed by the early Alpine people.

Indo-Aryan

The physical features of the Indo-Aryans were quite distinct from that of the earlier Australoids and Mediterraneans. They were taller than the latters. Their skin colour and eye colour were lighter. Their head hair was also not so dark. However, the Indo-Aryans were also dolichocephalic people, but their head was bigger in size and massive. The cranial capacity was also much higher than that of their predecessors. Their physique was robustly built.

The true representatives of the Indo-Aryans are the present day Baltic people inhabiting the southern part of the Hindukush. In India the Indo-Aryans are concentrated in the valleys of the Indus and the Ganges. In the Gangetic valley they are distributed upto western Bihar almost forming a continuous chain. Beyond that limit towards east, that is, in eastern Bihar, Bengal and Assam, their distribution is sporadic and in these regions the Indo-Aryan elements are mostly confined to the people of the upper castes. In this context it should be kept in mind that the physical characteristics of all the Indo-Aryans living in different parts of India are not the same, they show considerable variations among themselves. Moreover, the Indo-Aryan traits occur in varying degrees in varied populationss. To account for such situation, we can recall those factors like gene-flow, ecology, bio-social practices and so forth.

With the coming of Indo-Aryans, who are usually referred to as the Aryans, India witnessed the opening of a new chapter in her history with regard to development of a new civilization. The Indo-Aryans had a highly developed and distinctive culture of their own before entering India. They included people representing various vocations.

Most of them were expert agriculturists. The Indo-Aryans included groups of people who were specialised in cattle-breeding, that is, pastoral people. Some had the knowledge of metallurgy. Again, others specialised in ancestor-worship and eventually priest-craft. With the spread of the Brahmanic cult, in due course they became the intelligentsia group. A large number of copper, bronze and other materials have been discovered from different parts of Afghanistan, Indus and Gangetic valley, a methodical examination of which gives an indication that the Indo-Aryans entered India sometimes in 1200 B.C. However, possibility of earlier migration in small bands cannot be ruled out, though large scale migration occurred during the period mentioned. The migration started from Aral-Caspian region. We have already seen the spread of the Indo-Aryans to western Bihar. According to Chatterjee they arrived in northern Bihar at least by 700 B.C., if not earlier. From north Bihar they moved eastward in small groups at different intervals of time. Exactly at what time and how they entered Assam, is difficult to say with certainty.

The *Kalika Purana* tells us what Naraka drove away the Kiratas to the sea shore and gave settlement to the Dwija (Indo-Aryan Brahmins) in the region lying between Karatowa and Lalitakanta. It cannot be said with certainty who this Naraka was, as now it believed by some that there were several kings who were known as Naraka.

That Assam had early contact with the Indo-Aryans is borne out by the references in the *Ramayana* and the *Mahabharata.* Arjuna came to Manipur and married princess Chitrangada. Aniruddha married Usha, daughter of king Bana. All these suggest that Assam might have come under the influence of the Indo-Aryans from a very early period. But there was no large scale migration of the Indo-Aryans during that time.

The Dubi and Nidanpur copper-plates, of king Bhaskarvarman give us definite clue as regards the presence of Indo-Aryans in this part of the country, and that was in 7th century A.D. During his time Hiuen Tsiang, the Chinese pilgrim came to Kamrupa. In his records also we find that he met people of higher castes, Brahmin and Kayastha in the country ruled by Bhaskarvarman. Even during the time of Mahabhutivarman, the great grand father of Bhaskarvarman the Indo-Aryans represented by the Brahmins came to Assam.

We have already noted that before the coming of the Indo-Aryans to Assam, Mediterranean and small groups of some sort of Alpenoid people migrated to this part. Therefore, we can well imagine that there was an admixture among these three populationss.

In recent years another view regarding the original homeland of the Indo-Aryans and their movement to India is gaining popularity. According to some scholars the Indo-Aryans (Aryans) are very much of Indian origin. It is needless to look at outside India for locating their original habitat from where they are supposed to have migrated. These scholars have given several evidences to establish their view. Many of the evidences have been collected from Sanskrit literature and language. Cultural facts have also been added.

As examples, I wish to reproduce some quotations from the book titled *Aryo Ka Adidesh* written by Swami Vidyanand Saraswati, a stern advocate of the Indian origin of the Aryans, and who gave his own interpretations of some Sanskrit slokas to establish his view. "So far as I know, none of the Sanskrit books, not even the most ancient, contains any distinct reference or allusion to the foreign origin of the Aryans" (Muir). Elphinstone wrote, "neither in the code of Manu, nor in the Vedas, nor in any book which is older than the code of Monu, is there any allusion to the Aryan prior residence in any country outside India". "The Aryan invasion of India is recorded in no written document and it cannot yet be traced archaeologically." V.S. Vankankar claimed that "the Indus Valley Civilization script was original to India and its roots are found in the Aryan civilization". In *Hindustan Times* it was reported that "there is no evidence of Aryan immigration into India from outside..." The archaeological materials associated with Aryans in different regions did not show any links with the archaeological survival of the Aryans in Afghanisthan, Iran and Central Asia". Some scholars suggested that the Aryans came from Iran and Iraq. But Swamiji has pointed out that in the educational institutes of Iran the students are taught that the Aryans migrated to Iran from India.

Irano-Scythian

Sarkar (1958) has referred to another element in the populations of India and that is termed as the Irano-Scythian. They perhaps entered India almost at the same time with the Indo-Aryans. They migrated towards south along the western coast. According to some, these people were responsible for bringing Iron culture to India.

The long-headed Indo-Aryans were extended upto western Bihar. The dolichocephalic head was replaced by mesocephalic head in eastern Bihar, Bengal, Assam and the neighbouring areas. The people of this region are medium statured. According to Sarkar medium stature and mesocephalic head are the contribution of the Irano-Scythians.

This type of physical features are met with in the populations of western coast of India like

Gujarat, Bombay, Maharashtra. They spread as far as south. They were closely associated with the Megalithic culture of south as indicated by the unearthed materials.

A genetic relation could perhaps be established between the mesocephalic of western coast and those of Bengal. They probably migrated from the western coast to Bengal following the river valleys of the Narbada and the Son. This route was followed by the Marhatta plunders also.

The Irano-Scythian are quite distinct from the Indo-Aryans. They had ethnic affiliation with the people of Persia. The Kurd of modern time inhabiting certain regions of Persia are the true representatives of this type. The high mesocephaly and brachycephaly of western India appear to be due to this type.

The mesocephalic extended to as far as Assam. It is, however, not definitely known at what time did they come to Assam. The Indo-Aryans and the Irano-Scythians came almost at the same time to India, or may be the second type came a bit late. The Indo-Aryans followed the course of the Ganges spreading as far as western Bihar. On the other hand, the Irano-Scythians followed the western route and migrated south. One batch moved towards Bengal, from where this element entered to Assam. Of these two types, namely, the Indo-Aryans and Irano-Scythians, which one came to

Assam first is not known. But it seems to be a fact that among the present day Assamese Irano-Scythian elements predominate.

The Irano-Scythians are medium headed people, often showing tendency towards broad head. They are medium statured. The nose is mostly mesorrhine. These we have already noted. An anthropometric survey carried on by us (Das et al. 1980) reveals that the Assamese caste people are by and large medium statured. About 56, 50, 64, 56, 65 and 61 per cent of the Assamese Brahmin, Kalita, Kumar, Jogi, Hira and Kaibarta are medium-headed respectively. The mean index of all these castes is mesocephalic. Again, the Brahmins, Kalitas, Kumars, Jogis, Hiras and Kaibartas exhibit about 39, 52, 61, 66, 60 and 76 per cent of mesorrhine nose respectively. The nose of the Assamese Muslims is also mesorrhine in average, its percentage being about 69. Their head is mesocephalic, its percentage being about 48. They are short to medium statured. Hence, it can perhaps be said that of all the Caucasoid varieties that have entered into the populations of Assam, the Irano-Scythian and Mediterranean elements appear to be more conspicuous in the Assamese people of the present time.

SUMMARY

It may be summarised this way that the Australoids first came to Assam. Then came the

Mongoloids who partially or fully absorbed the old Australoid strains. The Mongoloids came from different directions and at different times. Though the migration of the Mongoloids was a continues process, yet it can be said that after the Mongoloids came the Caucasoids from the western direction. The Caucasoid migration also occurred in successive waves. Before the arrivals of the Indo-Aryans and Irano-Scythians, the Mediterraneans and Alpino-Armenoids came to this region.

Thus, as already has been mentioned, it is justified to say that Assam is a meeting place of the Mongoloids and Caucasoids. In many parts of this region, people belonging to these two major races are living side by side since long past. As a result, admixture in varying degrees has taken place between the members of the two groups. In some cases it is not easy to distinguish a man of Mongoloid origin from that of Caucasoid origin by observing their physical features.

Thus, a glance at the racial elements in the populations of Assam reveals that Assam is a meeting place of various ethnic stocks having diverse socio-cultural backgrounds who came to this part of the country in different times from different directions. In the course of time these populationss contributed their respective shares towards the growth and development of a composite Assamese people and culture.

Chapter 4
Ongoing Processes in Assam

Anthropological approach to the study of ethnic elements and human populations has undergone significant changes during the last few decades with the addition on new knowledge to anthropology and allied subjects as well as new methodology and technology. Human populations groups are not static units, but are liable to change on account of several factors, both cultural and biological and interaction between the two. Populations dynamics, microvariation, microevolutionary trends, etc., have attracted attention more and more of the anthropologists. These sort of subjects help in understanding certain basic facts of populations genetics and formulating new hypotheses and testing them. Anthropologists have identified four basic factors responsible for changing morphological traits and also gene frequencies in human populations. These are mutation, selection, gene flow and genetic drift. There are several other agencies like migration, isolation, founder effect, mating system and similar other cultural factors which may accelerate or otherwise the functioning of these four principal factors.

In what follows, it is proposed to give briefly and in a general way some ideas about certain processes, mentioned above, operating among some populationss of Assam, so that a reader can examine in these perspectives before accepting, rejecting or modifying what have been discussed in chapter three.

It has been demonstrated by several anthropologists taking samples from various populationss of different parts of the globe at different times that after a considerable period the descendants of the immigrants exhibited differences in certain morphological traits, though may be in smaller magnitude, from their progenitors who continued to live in their original habitat. Anthropometric measurements and somatoscopie observations are traits of continuous variation. These are determined by several loci, that means, these may be regarded as polygenic. Any effect on the polygenic system produces different forms. Hence, these traits appear to be plastic in nature.

Various sections of the same ancestral group, when distributed over larger geographic area and continue to live under different types of environment may undergo certain changes and exhibit microdifferentiations among them. This may be described as regional variation. Again, in some cases different sections of the same group living in the same region may also show such microvariations among themselves because of several factors including biological isolation. Some such groups of the same ethnic origin can be arranged in such a manner so as to demonstrate microevolutionary trends. As a result of these processes the populations cannot always remain static, they exhibit changes in their morphological type, the racial criteria—the bases of identifying ethnic elements.

It is not that variations occur only in case of morphological traits. The same is true as regards gene frequency as well. As a matter of fact changes or differences in gene frequencies can be proved more clearly and accurately.

These sort of ongoing processes of variation and microevolution are very much on operation among several populationss of Assam, which have been recognizably established by various workers. Instead of going into the detailed discussion of those works here, a few examples will be cited and that too, in a very general way avoiding the technical aspects. Before that once again let us recollect the major factors for bringing variation, namely, mutation, selection, gene flow and genetic drift as well as the other factors like migration, founder effect, isolation and so forth. In the present context perhaps it will not make any differences if not much importance is given to mutation and genetic drift. But the role played by the other factors cannot be ignored. The examples which we are going to incorporate will obviously illustrate the effectiveness of the various factors, just mentioned, in different situations.

Biology and Culture

We mentioned about interaction between biological and cultural factors. As a matter of fact it is regarded that the interaction between these two factors determine the course of human evolution. Cultural capability is a part of the biology of man. However, culture passes from one generation to another in society through socialization, while biology does so through genes, or in other words as a result of sexual intercourse or mating patterns. The mating patterns or marriage regulations are again prescribed by the society. Hence, socio - cultural variables, for example, religion, language, nationality, occupation, caste system, etc., play significant role in human populations variation. It is needless to emphasis that socio-cultural changes is a continuous process. Some changing patterns will undoubtedly have significant effect on the biology of man.

All these processes, however, affect the biology of man very slowly. The results become discernible after a considerably long time. The time required to bring about changes in biology is very long in comparison to that for producing cultural changes in a populations. The changes in culture are more apparent than that in biology.

Geography plays an important role in keeping the populations in isolation. Modern communication and transport facilities have lifted the geographic barrier to a great extent. Industrial development, rapid spread of education, growth of cities, etc., have brought the various populationss more and more closer. Social changes also helped in breaking down biological isolation. The marriage distances in terms of space are gradually increasing thereby bringing changes in the local isolates.

MICROEVOLUTION AND MICROVARIATION

Evolution may be regarded as the development of differences between the ancestral and descendant populationss. The differences may be in respect of morphological traits as well as gene frequencies. Here it should perhaps be clearly stated that in the present context we are not discussing about macroevolution, but dealing with microevolution. That means such differences between two concerned populations are very minute and to identify these differences, careful observation, precision technique and application of proper statistical method are necessary.

South Goalpara

In the earlier chapter we have mentioned the evidences to establish the fact that the ancestors of the Garos, Rạbhas and Kacharis belong to the same original stock. To be more precise so far the erstwhile South Goalpara is concerned, we can add to these three populationss one more, known as the Rajbanshis, because as has already been mentioned earlier, persons originally belonging to tribes after conversion to Hinduism are given the name Rajbanshi. These populations of South Goalpara were studied by the present writer in late fifties, and also subsequently, and found that they show biological variation in such manners that they could be arranged in a way so as to demonstrate micro-evolutionary trend among them. The results can be summarized in a general way as follows. From the Garo 'base-line' to the 'end-product' Rajbanshi through the intermediate group Rabha-Kachari, the stature has increased; the face has become relatively longer and narrower; the head has become broader and shorter; and the nose has become longer and narrower. As regards somatoscopic characters, from the Garos to the Rajbanshis through the Rabha-Kachari the frequency of scanty growth of beard and moustache has decreased; the frequency of coarse and smooth head hair has decreased, but that of wavy hair has increased; the lips have shown a tendency towards thinner size; prominence of zygomatic arch has become lesser. Eye slit has become straight, palpebral fissure wide and mongoloid fold less marked. The Garos are sturdy people, and that sturdiness have been maintained by the Rabhas and Kacharis to some extent, while the Rajbanshis are of slender built.

In respect of percentile occurrence of finger ridge patterns, the Rajbanshis differ significantly from each of the three tribes, by showing whorl and loop in the ratio of 43 : 54, whereas among the Garos and Rabhas the ratio is almost 50 : 50, but in the Kacharis it is about 55 : 43. Thus, the Kacharis also differ from the Garos as well as the Rabhas in this respect.

As regards ABO blood groups, the four populationss do not show significant variations among them, though the Garo-Rajbanshi and Rabha-Rajbanshi values are significant at 5 per cent level. B is more frequent among the Kacharis and Rajbanshis, while among the Garos and Rabhas A and B occur almost in equal frequencies. Rh-negative factor rarely occurs among the Mongoloids. It was found in 0.79 per cent only among the Rabhas, but the Rajbanshis have it in 3.25 per cent. All the Garo and Kachari individuals tested by us were Rh-positive.

Let us make an attempt to account for the development of this type of variation among these four populationss, which have originated from the same source. In this connection perhaps it may be mentioned that human ethics as well as government laws do not permit to carry on certain experiment on man in Anthropology unlike on animals in Zoology, on plants in Botany, etc. Therefore, very often it is difficult to isolate each and every factors affecting the different ongoing processes in man. A host of factors may be involved in one event, the relative importance of them can only be pointed out in certain cases.

In chapter three we have already stated that the ancestors of the Rabha, Garo and Kachari migrated to Assam in succession. Each batch established settlement in different areas—some were isolated from one another, some were in adjoining areas, and in some cases there were overlapping of areas. In course of time each assumed a name and formed a group or tribe. Each one of them became endogamous, that means biological isolation started. But each of them had its own biological endowment, which may be called biological foundation of the tribe. In other words founder effect also played its role.

The four populations can be divided into three ecological categories. *Firstly*, the Garos who are essentially a hill people living in the hills, though some of them have settled in the plains also. *Secondly*, the Rajbanshis and Kacharis are plains people, their villages being located in the plains region of the river valleys. The Rabhas can be regarded to represent the third category, because a section of them like to live in small hillocks.

Again, looking at from the point of view of the process of detribalization, these four populationss are found to be in three different stages. *Firstly*, the Garos living in their own hilly territory were preserving to a great extent their traditional way life. *Secondly*, the Rajbanshis formed a completely detribalized group. They had already a Hindu caste name. Their way of life was more or less the same as that of their neighbouring Hindu castes. *Thirdly*, the Rabhas and Kacharis represented a stage, which may be called a transitional one. The Garos are matriarchal people, the Kacharis and Rajbanshis are patriarchal, while the Rabhas are in transition from matriarchy to patriarchy.

Thus, very briefly it can be said that the ancestors of the three tribes migrated to different places, settled under various environmental conditions, became isolated biologically from each other retaining its founder effect. The Rajbanshis emerged out of these three tribes on account of certain socio-cultural factors and became an endogamous caste. The isolation, however, could not continue to be so rigid. Infiltration of genes started from one populations to another on different occasions under different circumstances. Thus, all these factors contributed their respective shares to cause variation among these populationss. Certain processes are still continuing in different magnitudes and in different manners.

Kachari

Phookan (1972) studied four divisions of the Kacharis, namely, the Dimasa, Jharua, Sonowal and Thengal, from the point of view of microvariation. The Dimasas mostly live in the North Cachar hills and geographically isolated from the other three, which are occupying contiguous areas in the river valleys of Upper Assam districts. He found that the Dimasas are slightly different from the rest in their physical make up. They are shorter in stature; their head is longer and narrower; face and nose are shorter, etc. With regard to ABO blood groups also, they differ from the other three showing occurrence of high B gene. Most of the factors mentioned in connection with the people of South Goalpara may be taken into account to explain such variation among the Kachari tribe.

Garo

We have found that the Garos are basically a hill people. But a section of them since long past is living in the plains. Thus, according to their habitat two sections of the Garos namely, Hill Garo and Plains Garo, can be recognized. However, it cannot be said that the two sections are completely separated from one another forming two different tribal groups. But for various socio-cultural and geographical reasons the members of each prefer to marry within the group. The present writer (1960) examined certain anthropometric traits of these two sections of the Garos and observed differences between the two. The Plains Garos are significantly taller than the Hill Garos; their face and nose are longer and narrower, etc. In this case though ecological factor or geography appears to play stronger role, yet certain other factors like gene flow also deserve careful examination.

Chutiya

Of the several sections of the Chutiyas of Upper Assam districts we (Das 1981) looked at two—the Deuri Chutiyas and the Hindu Chutiyas. One tends to differ from the other in certain physical anthropological characters. The Deuri Chutiyas, being the priestly section of the Chutiyas consider themselves responsible for preserving their socio-cultural heritage and they marry among themselves thus forming some sort of closed society. On the other hand, the Hindu Chutiyas are very much like the other Hindu castes. The possibility of exchange of genetic traits between the Hindu Chutiyas and the other neighbouring people cannot be denied. Hence, socio-cultural factors appear to help in separating one section from the other, and thereby to form two different isolates.

Man

The Man populations of the Garo hills studied by Sanjib Chakravarty (1982) is a nice example of microevolutionary dynamics. The founder members of this Man populations came from Burma during the first quarter of the nineteenth century when the Burmese invaded Assam. They were soldiers and all of them were male. When some of them decided to stay back in Assam they had to marry local girls belonging to the Garos, Rabhas, Kochs, Hajongs, etc., and hence gene started flowing from these groups to the original Man populations making it a hybrid people. Now the Mans form an endogamous unit, though endogamy is not practised very strictly. Genetic markers like ABO, MN, Rh, sector status, taste sensitivity to PTC, etc., were examined by Chakravarty to illustrate the microevolutionary dynamics in them. At present the Mans are genetically separated from their ancestral stock, the Shan people of Burma, but are closer to the Boro and the allied peoples.

Khasi

The present writer reported microevolutionary trends as observed among the four divisions of the Khasi, namely, Khynriam, Pnar, War and Bhoi (1978). I would like to quote from my book : "An analysis of the anthropometric data reveals significant interdivision differences in respect of many characteristics. Only the Khynriam and the War are very similar to one another. The differences among the four divisions indicate that the Khasi tribe is, at present, not a homogeneous populations. We can assume that each of the divisions is showing a tendency to separate from the original stock with common Khasi characteristics, and that each of these more or less endogamous groups is heading towards acquiring a somewhat different physique. The separating tendency is more pronounced in the Bhoi and Pnar than in the other two divisions."

On the other hand, we do not see the same picture with regard to other parameters like ABO blood groups, dermatoglyphics and taste sensitivity to PTC. There appears to have a common agreement among the Khynriam, Pnar and War in respect of these. They do not deviate significantly from the Khasi tribe as a whole. This suggests that the interdivision variability is more in respect of metric characters than in respect of genetic traits, (In this context we can recollect the plastic nature of the anthropometric traits).

The position of the Bhoi is, however, different. They deviate significantly from the other divisions as well as the Khasi tribe as a whole, not only in respect of anthropometry, but also in respect of ABO blood groups, finger patterns and taste sensitivity to PTC. Thus, the Bhois appear to have already formed a separate biological unit.

We must admit that we cannot with certainty account for such situation among the Khasi division. But perhaps we can visualize certain possibilities. Though each of the Khasi divisions is not theoretically endogamous yet because of geographic and socio-cultural factors, in practice they prefer to marry within the sub-division, which has led to some sort of biological isolation. The Bhoi habitat lies in lower altitude and towards north the altitude of the Khasi hills gradually decreases to meet the Brahmaputra plain, where other tribes also inhabit. In such a situation there is great possibility of gene flow from the neighbouring tribes to the Bhois.

REGIONAL VARIATION

The Assamese Hindu castes and Muslims are spread all over Assam, more particularly in the plains region. A study was conducted by us (Das *et al* 1985, 1986) among a few castes as well as the Muslims in order to investigate into certain aspects of physical anthropology including regional variation. The sample were collected from the rural areas of the different erstwhile districts of the Brahmaputra valley. Here some relevant results obtained from the study will be incorporated to highlight regional variation exhibited by these populationss.

Kalita

The Kalitas of five erstwhile districts, namely, Goalpara, Kamrup, Nagaon, Darrang and Sibsagar, show more or less marked and statistically significant variation in respect of head and face measurements, stature, ABO blood groups, taste sensitivity to PTC, dermatoglyphic and behavioural traits. The Kalita as a caste is no doubt endogamous, but in practice most of the marriages took place within a small radius of the same district, and hence the Kalitas of each district can be regarded as endogamous units. This suggests that gene flow among the various Kalita groups (district group) is considerably low. Besides this lack of extensive genetic contacts among them, one is to consider certain locally acting factors like drift and/or founder effect. Moreover, though this has not been proved by our study, yet gene flow to the Kalitas of each district from the respective populations who live nearby cannot be ruled out. Thus, gene flow might be another reason to cause variation.

Brahmin

In comparison to the Kalitas, marked and significant variability is generally much less among the Brahmins of three districts, namely, Kamrup, Darrang and Sibsagar. Among the Brahmins variabilities are observed with regard to upper facial index, total facial index, nasal index, taste sensitivity to PTC and some behavioural traits. Nevertheless, it cannot perhaps be said that the three Assamese Brahmin groups are anthropologically uniform. The situation may be explained by more or less the same factors as in the case of Kalitas.

Kaibarta

The Kaibartas of five districts, that is, Goalpara, Kamrup, Nagaon, Darrang and Dibrugarh were also examined from this angle. The results may be summarized as follows : Interdistrict variation is negligible in respect of dermatoglyphics. Differences are not significant with regard to taste sensitivity to PTC also almost in all the cases. In respect of ABO blood groups, the Kaibartas of Darrang stand markedly apart from those of the other districts, among whom variabilities are not that noteworthy. In most of the behavioural traits interdistrict variations are remarkable. As regards anthropometric traits variabilities are more than that in dermatoglyphic and genetic traits. Thus, regional variations occur among the Kaibartas also though not to that extent as in the Kalitas.

Muslim

The Assamese Muslim samples were collected from six districts and these are Goalpara, Kamrup, Darrang, Nagaon, Sibsagar and Dibrugarh. The study revealed more or less marked and significant variations among the six Muslim groups. The Muslims of Dibrugarh are, however, obviously different from those of the other districts in many traits, for example, some indices, finger ridge patterns, ABO blood groups, behavioural traits, etc., while among the other five intergroup variability is comparatively less. Taking into account the historical and socio-cultural background, it is not very difficult to give reasons for this situation. The Dibrugarh sample consists of the Marias, to which reference has already been made in the first chapter, while the others belong to the Sheikh section. The Marias are having a rather low social position in the Assamese Muslim society and they marry among themselves (Ahmed, Das, 1977).

The geographical environment of the Sheikh is more or less the same as they are inhabiting different regions of the same Brahmaputra valley. But the ethnic environment varies from region to region. It has already been stated in the first chapter that many local people were converted to Islam time to time. Therefore, if the local populations vary anthropologically, then it is easily presumable that the Muslims who included local converts will also show regional variation. But at the same time we must not forget the factors operating in the case of the castes of produce variability.

Perhaps it will not be out of context if we quote what Farida Ahmed Das has brought to light about the Muslims of Dibrugarh through her work among them. She wrote : "The three groups (Garia, Maria and Bihari Muslims) do not form a single homogeneous Muslim unit. A relative homogeneity is, however, observed in the case of the Garia and Maria in respect of a number of metric and genetic traits. Thus, the Garia and Maria are different from the Bihari Muslim and maintain a separate identity as the Assamese Muslim". She has given reason: "The Bihari Muslim marry exclusively within their group or from among the Muslim of the places of their origin. They have not yet been Assamised either culturally or biologically." She has also noted differences between the Garia (Sheikh) and Maria.

Meitei

A bioanthropological study of three populationss, namely, Meitei (Manipui Kshatriya), Khangabok (Bishnupriya) and Andro (scheduled caste), of the Manipur valley has also revealed genetic variation, both inter and intra, among them with regard to blood groups, PTC taste sensitivity, dermatoglyphic and anthropometric traits (Singh, 1978).

ADMIXTURE

In chapter three we have already observed that various populationss, of Caucasoid and Mongoloid origins have been living together from time immemorial in Assam. The representatives of each of the two major races, however, are still preserving their physical anthropological identities to a great extent. As a racial group one is undoubtedly distinguishable from the other even by naked eye observation. The same is true at the populations level, that means, when one Mongoloid populations is compared with a Caucasoid populations. But at the individual level in many cases the differences completely or partially disappear, which means that a man of Mongoloid origin cannot always be distinguished from that of Caucasoid origin by the physical features, and *vice versa.* A man may consider himself judging from his physical appearance a good representative of the Indo-Aryan group, but he may not know that he has in him a good number of biological traits which have come from the Mongoloid stock.

ABO Blood Groups

Several Caucasoid and Mongoloid populations were investigated for ABO blood groups on different occasions by us. More than one sample on ABO blood groups are available on the same populations. The samples on the same populations have not been pooled. The distribution of phenotypes and gene frequencies in different populations are given in Table 3.

When the populations are grouped according to gene frequencies in the order of O>B>A and O>A>B, it is seen that all the Caucasoid Hindu castes, Muslim and also Rajbanshi belong to the first group. But in case of the Mongoloid populations no such uniformity is observed. The Garo, Boro, Jharua, Dimasa and Moran fall under O>B>A category and the Sonowal, Thengal, Deuri, Kachari, Mishing and Khasi belong to the other group, i.e., O>A>B. Again, in case of the Rabha, Tiwa, Chutiya, Karbi and Ahom, where more than one sample are available, on the basis of some sample they belong to O>A>B group and according to other they are under O>B>A group. Thus, though the Caucasoid populations are similar to certain Mongoloid populations and differ from others, yet among themselves similarity is observed in respect of pattern of distribution of O, B and A.

On the basis of another type of criterion, the populations have been grouped in the following manner.

Group I : Predominance of O (above 0.6), with

high A and low B. Chutiya, Khasi, Rajbanshi (1), Ahom (3), Kachari (3), Sonowal (3).

Group II : Predominance of O (above 0.6), with high B and low A. Brahmin (2), Kalita (1, 2), Kayastha, Keot, Baishya, Kumar, Jogi, Hira, Kaibarta (1), Muslim, Ahom (1). Kalita (3), Kaibarta (3), Rajbanshi (3), Muslim (3), Chutiya (3).

Group III : Populationss with O (below 0.6), high A and low B, Rabha (1), Sonowal, Thengal, Tiwa (1), Karbi (2), Deuri, Khasi (2), Mishing.

Group IV : Populations with O (below 0.6) high B and low A. Brahmin (1), Kaibarta (2), Rajbanshi (2), Rabha (2), Garo, Boro, Jharua, Dimasa, Tiwa (2), Karbi (1), Moran, Ahom (2), Brahmin (3), Karbi (3).

A more or less similar picture is presented by this type of grouping also. All the Caucasoid populations, except a few samples, show predominance of O with high B and low A. As in case of the earlier type of grouping, the Mongoloid populations are distributed under all the Groups.

But perhaps in general it could be said that some sort of difference is observed in between the Caucasoid and Mongoloid populations with regard to the qualitative pattern of distribution of ABO blood group gene frequencies.

In Fig. 2, the values are plotted. The Caucasoid

populations appear to concentrate at the central region, whereas the Mongoloid populationss are distributed around the Caucasoids, showing greater distances among them.

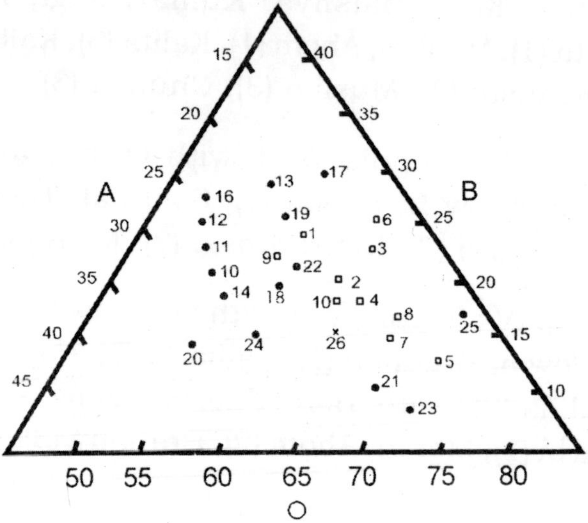

Fig. 2 ABO blood groups.

1. Brahmin	8. Hira	15. Thengal	22. Moran
2. Kalita	9. Kaibarta	16. Jharua	23. Khasi
3. Kayastha	10. Muslim	17. Dimasa	24. Mishing
4. Keot	11. Rabha	18. Tiwa	25. Ahom
5. Baishya	12. Garo	19. Karbi	26. Rajbanshi
6. Kumar	13. Boro	20. Deuri	
7. Jogi	14. Sonowal	21. Chutiya	

Table 3.* Distribution of ABO Phenotypes (in %) and Allele Frequencies

Populationss	*N*	*Phenotypes*				*Allele Frequenceis*		
		O	*A*	*B*	*AB*	*p(A)*	*q(B)*	*r(O)*
1	*2*	*3*	*4*	*5*	*6*	*7*	*8*	*9*
Brahmin (1)	536	35.6	21.6	32.8	10.0	.172	.242	.586
Brahmin (2)	360	38.6	23.0	33.0	5.5	.157	.214	.628
Kalita (1)	895	37.9	23.9	30.5	7.7	.173	.214	.613
Kalita (2)	454	38.5	24.2	31.2	5.9	.165	.208	.626
Kayastha	492	40.0	20.9	32.9	6.3	.148	.220	.632
Keot	138	35.5	23.1	26.0	15.2	.174	.193	.633
Baishya	145	48.2	22.7	24.8	4.1	.146	.158	.696
Kumar	202	34.1	21.8	41.1	3.0	.134	.256	.610
Jogi	411	43.8	25.5	26.3	4.4	.164	.168	.668
Kaibarta (1)	532	32.1	28.6	31.2	8.1	.205	.222	.573
Kaibarta (2)	161	40.3	11.8	44.0	3.7	.078	.274	.642
Hira	266	47.4	20.7	24.8	7.1	.149	.174	.677
Muslim	837	40.0	25.1	25.7	9.2	.188	.192	.620
Rabha (1)	600	25.5	32.5	29.8	12.2	.257	.238	.506
Rabha (2)	126	24.6	30.9	31.7	12.7	.249	.254	.494
Garo	144	25.6	28.8	32.6	11.8	.236	.255	.507
Boro Kachari	132	26.5	23.4	40.9	9.0	.180	.294	.525
Sonowal Kachari	100	30.0	34.0	24.0	12.0	.264	.198	.537
Thengal Kachari	100	28.0	33.0	26.0	13.0	.266	.217	.518
Jharua								

Kachari Dimasa	100	28.0	24.0	30.0	18.0	.233	.272	.493
Kachari	100	32.0	16.0	41.0	11.0	.144	.305	.550
Tiwa (1)	94	29.9	32.9	31.9	5.2	.217	.211	.570
Tiwa (2)	114	33.3	26.3	31.5	8.7	.194	.227	.577
Deuri	200	28.5	44.0	19.5	8.0	.309	.149	.542
Karbi (1)	200	26.5	31.0	38.0	4.5	.201	.266	.540
Karbi (2)	134	30.6	32.8	28.3	8.2	.233	.204	.561
Chutiya	184	47.3	31.5	16.9	4.3	.200	.112	.688
Moran	200	32.0	29.0	31.5	7.5	.204	.220	.576
Mishing	196	32.7	38.3	21.4	7.6	.265	.158	.577
Ahom (1)	202	52.0	25.7	17.3	5.0	.167	.188	.715
Ahom (2)	130	38.4	23.8	26.1	11.5	.193	.207	.598
Khasi (1)	821	48.6	30.4	16.7	4.3	.193	.108	.700
Khasi (2)	136	33.8	34.5	25.0	6.6	.234	.174	.591
Rajbanshi Koch (1)	527	37.3	30.3	26.7	5.5	.200	.178	.621
Rajbanshi - Koch (2)	166	37.3	17.4	33.7	11.4	.154	.256	.589

* Reproduce from 'The Brahmaputra Valley Population, by the Author.

Haemoglobin E

Haemoglobin E (HbβE) is the only haemoglobin variant, which occurs in appreciable frequencies in the people of Assam, and also this is the only haemoglobin variant so far detected among the autochthons of this region. Till 1971 little was known about the distribution of HbβE in Northeast

India, except mention of sporadic cases in Assam and an indication of high prevalence of this gene in the Toto tribe inhabiting the Assam Bengal border, who have approximately 23 per cent HbβE carriers. The association of high frequencies of HbβE with people of the Austroasiatic language group in Southeast Asia (Flatz et al, 1965) led to the study of the Khasi, an Austroasiatic tribe and some other populationss of Assam (Das et al, 1971: Flatz et al, 1972). Thus, began the first phase of systematic works on the distribution of HbβE in Assam. Initially three populationss were investigated. These are : the Khasi; the Ahom, descendants of a Tai group who migrated to Assam in the 13th century and the Assamese caste populations.

The first publication of this study showed a high frequency of HbβE gene (0.219) in the Khasi, and a still higher frequency of 0.359 in the Ahom. The second publication confirmed the earlier findings of high prevalence of the gene in these populationss. The high frequency of the gene in the Khasi was in support of the hypothesis of a correlation between Austroasiatic linguistic affiliation and in high prevalence of HbβE. The higher prevalence of the gene among the Ahom led to much speculation.

The Assamese sample, which included some Caucasoid Hindu castes and also a few Muslim individuals, presented a somewhat lower but still considerable frequency of HbβE gene (0.107). This Assamese sample was from Lower Assam. In 1975 another similar Assamese sample was drawn from Upper Assam. There are frequency of HbβE gene (0.135) was a little higher, though the difference between the two samples was not statistically significant. These Caucasoid Assamese have no doubt acquired this gene from the neighbouring Mongoloid populationss where HbβE occurs in high frequency.

In the second study (Flatz et al, 1972) mentioned above, five Kachari individuals of the Tibeto-Burman language family were also examined. All of them were found to be carriers of HbβE, either being heterozygous or homozygous. This gave an indication that the distribution of HbβE, in Assam is not limited to those populations only, who have direct connection to Southeast Asia. Therefore, in 1975 (Das et al) a large number of Kachari individuals were tested for HbbE. Among them the gene frequency of HbβE was found to be very high (0.509). This observation required special attention in view of the fact that till 1967 very little or no HbβE was detected in any Tibeto-Burman group of Southeast Asia (Flatz 1967).

Now several sets of data on different

populations groups are available. These are included in Table 4, which reveals a characteristic pattern of distribution of HbβE gene in the populations of Assam. The Caucasoid Assamese Hindu castes and Muslims show lower frequencies than in the Mongoloid populations. Of the castes again the Brahmin show the lowest frequency (0.051). Of the Mongoloid groups the Boro and the allied tribes show very high frequencies. The lowest frequencies are observed among the Khasi, Karbi and Chutiya. In between these two extremes lie the Ahom. It may be assumed that the HbβE gene entered into the Caucasoid populations by gene flow from the Mongoloid populations. Again, higher frequency of this gene in the Assamese of Upper Assam, in comparison with the Assamese of Lower Assam, perhaps reflect the presumably more infiltration by the Mongoloids in this area. It may be noted that the frequency in the Kaibarta is very similar to that in the Assamese of Upper Assam.

The situation with regard to the frequency of HbβE gene in the Rajbanshi (0.350) deserves special consideration. Their position is intermediate between the Caucasoid and Mongoloid populations. Three Rajbanshi samples were drawn from three different regions : (A) from western part of Kamrup district where they are living alongwith some tribes like the Rabha, Garo and Kachari of the Tibeto-Burman group with high frequency of HbβE; (B) from Nagaon district, where their settlement is very close to the Tiwa tribe among whom HbbE occurs in high frequency; (C) near Guwahati where they are surrounded by the Assamese castes having relatively low frequency of HbβE Thus, it appears that the highest frequency of HbβE (0.456) is shown by the Rajbanshi who live with the Boro tribes followed by the Rajbanshi of Tiwa area (0.434), and the lowest frequency (0.229) by the Rajbanshi surrounded by caste populations. It may be noted that a similar pattern of descending order in the frequency of this gene is observed from the Boro tribes to the Tiwa and then to the Assamese castes. There is not statistically significant difference between A and B samples, while C sample differs significantly from A as well as B. This suggests that the Rajbanshi of the Mongoloid tribal areas are descendants of recent converts and as such are still preserving HbβE gene in high frequencies. On the other hand, the Rajbanshi of C area show 'dilution' of HbβE frequency by admixture with the Caucasoid caste populations.

This discloses another interesting phenomenon of which mention was made in chapter one, and that is, tribe-caste continuum. We have pointed out to the fact time and again that the Rajbanshis or Kochs are of Mongoloid tribal origin. They constitute a detribalized group which have been forged out of several tribal societies and now form an integral part of the Assamese caste society. This is an ongoing process as a result of which tribal people are entering into the caste fold of the Assamese Hindu society. We have already noted that in the field of biology also, they have acquired a type different from their ancestors. It is needless to emphasise the socio-cultural elements in them.

*** Table 4 : Distribution of Haemoglobin Types (in %) and HbβE Allele Frequency**

Populations	*Place*	*No*	*Haemoglobin*		*Type*	*Allele Frequency*
			A A	*AE*	*EE*	*HbβE*
1	2	3	4	5	6	7
Rabha	Lower Assam	128	18.7	55.4	25.7	0.535
Garo	"	135	31.8	37.0	31.3	0.496
Kachari	"	131	21.3	47.3	31.3	0.549
Kachari	Upper Assam	555	24.1	49.7	26.1	0.509
Kachari	Lower Assam	110	16.3	38.1	45.4	0.645
Tiwa	"	114	29.8	50.8	19.3	0.447
Sonowal	Upper Assam	106	37.7	45.2	16.9	0.396
Karbi	Lower Assam	131	66.4	27.4	6.1	0.198
Karbi	"	110	62.7	29.0	8.2	0.227

Khasi	Meghalaya	80	58.5	38.7	2.5	0.219
Khasi	”	140	59.2	36.4	4.2	0.225
Chutiya	Upper Assam	62	46.7	46.7	6.4	0.298
Rajbanshi A	Lower Assam	46	32.6	43.8	23.9	0.456
Rajbanshi B	”	46	30.4	52.1	17.3	0.434
Rajbanshi C	”	72	62.5	29.1	8.3	0.229
Rajbanshi (A+B+C)	”	164	45.1	37.6	15.2	0.350
Rajbanshi	”	102	58.8	36.2	4.9	0.230
Ahom	Upper Assam	89	52.8	41.5	5.6	0.264
Ahom	”	181	42.5	46.4	11.0	0.342
Ahom	”	129	41.8	46.5	11.6	0.349
Ahom	”	119	36.1	47.0	16.8	0.404
Ahom	”	82	41.6	45.1	13.4	0.359
Brahmin	Lower Assam	98	89.7	10.2	-	0.051
Kalita	”	104	78.8	19.2	1.9	0.115
Kaibarta	”	101	74.2	24.7	0.9	0.133
Muslim	”	104	80.7	18.2	0.9	0.101
Assamese	”	182	81.3	15.9	2.7	0.107
Assamese	Upper Assam	133	76.6	19.5	3.7	0.135

* Reproduced from “The Brahmaputra Valley Population” by the Author.

Cerumen Type

Matsunaga (1962) demonstrated considerable racial variation in the occurrence of the two phenotypic form of human cerumen (ear wax), namely, wet and dry types. Dry cerumen is highly frequent in the Mongoloid people, and it is considered to be a Mongoloid trait. Some other researches also obtained similar results. The present writer (1975, 1977) also examined certain populations of Assam, some of which are in general of Caucasoid origins and the others belong to the Mongoloid race.

The observed phenotypic frequencies of the two types of cerumen and the estimated gene frequencies of the recessive dry allele (q) as found in the various populationss of Assam are presented in Table 5. However, in the truest sense, the Monpas of Arunachal do not belong to Assam. Yet they have been included just to establish the fact that the dry type occurs in high frequencies in the Mongoloid population.

Among the Monpas the frequency of dry cerumen is as high as 97.1 per cent (q = 0.985). They have not come in closer contact with Caucasic people. The same is true in case of the Kuki (81.4%) and Hmar (82.1%) among whom the dry type occurs in very high frequencies. The Mishing (84.0%) and Ahom (85.0%) though live in the valley have retained this Mongoloid trait to a great extent.

An opposite picture is observed among the Caucasoid caste group, more particularly the general castes, where the frequencies of the wet type are quite high, though not as high as dry cerumen in the above mentioned five Mongoloid populations. It is around 72 per cent among these castes, whereas among the scheduled castes it is around 60 per cent. The Muslims occupy an intermediate position between these two, showing inclination to the latter.

We have already noted the position of the Rajbanshi (Koch). They agree with their ancestral populationss like the Rabha, Kachari, Garo and Hajong (χ^2 = 0.04; 0.90> p> 0.80) as well as total Tibeto-Burman. But they differ from the general caste. On the other, the Rajbanshi are similar to the Kaibarta, a scheduled caste.

Table 5*. Distribution of Cerumen Types (in %)

Populations	*N*	*Wet Type*	*Dry Type*	*Gene Frequency q (dry)*
Brahmin	232	72.4	27.6	0.525
Kalita	321	72.0	28.0	0.529
Kayastha	47	72.3	27.7	0.525

Kaibarta	69	58.0	42.0	0.648
Scheduled Caste	40	60.0	40.0	0.632
Muslim	114	64.9	5.1	0.592
Matak	105	4.8	56.2	0.749
Rabha	108	57.4	42.6	0.653
Boro Kachari	105	39.0	61.0	0.780
Garo	125	54.4	45.6	0.675
Hajong	125	47.2	52.8	0.727
Mishing	81	16.0	84.0	0.916
Ahom	260	15.0	85.0	0.922
Kuki	43	18.6	81.4	0.902
Hmar	67	17.9	82.1	0.906
Rajbanshi Koch (Assam)	54	48.1	51.9	0.720
Rajbanshi Koch (Meghalaya)	111	51.4	48.6	0.698
Monpa (Arunachal)	70	2.9	97.1	0.985

* Reproduced from 'The Brahmaputra Valley Population' by the Author.

Haddon (1924) included the Boro group under the Protomorphus group of the Mesocephals division of the Asiatic Xanthoderms. He wrote "it is probable that this group is more allied to the leucoderms than to the Xanthoderms". In average, in the Tibeto-Burman group wet (49.7%) and dry (50.3%) types occur in equal percentages. A similar picture is noticed among the Koch (Rajbanshi) populations of Meghalaya, where it is regarded as a tribe and also of Assam, where the Koch are akin to the Boro populations as well as the caste populations. The Matak is a heterogeneous populations in the sense that people of both Mongoloid and Caucasoid origins having the same religious faith had formed this group. In them the two types of cerumen occur in almost equally high frequencies.

Among the Kaibartas the frequency of wet type is rather low in comparison to that in the other caste populations. The present writer (1973) once discussed the possibility of flow of gene from the Mongoloid populations to the Kaibartas. Das (1979) has shown that the Kaibartas differ in respect of many biological traits from the Brahmins and Kalitas.

A careful scrutiny of the data not only reveals marked ethnic difference in the relative frequencies of the cerumen types among the various populationss, but also help in determining their relative positions, which may be considered as an indicative of admixture. Hence, it could perhaps be said that the cerumen could be used as a genetic marker for populations study, more particularly in a region like northeast India where Caucasoids and Mongoloids live side by side.

SUMMARY

Anyway, our purpose was to demonstrate that the Caucasoid and Mongoloid groups have maintained their respective physical anthropological identities to a great extent, but at the same time they are exchanging genes among themselves. The above examples of ABO blood groups, haemoglobin variant HbβE and cerumen type perhaps adequately support these facts.

To this reference may be made to the work of Danker-Hopfe et al (1988) who demonstrated the relations among 13 populations of Assam with respect to anthropometric traits, behavioural traits, finger ridge patterns, ABO blood groups and PTC taste sensitively simultaneously as shown in Fig. 3.

The figure shows that the Caucasoid Brahmin, Kalita, Kaibarta, Sheikh, Kumar, Jogi and Hira form one main cluster, while the other cluster includes the Mongoloid Ahom, Chutiya, Moran, Mishing and Deuri and also the Maria. The populations of the two major groups are distinctly differentiated except the Maria. The Brahmin and Kalita, members of the general caste, form one sub-cluster. The Kaibarta and Sheikh Muslim form another sub-cluster. The Kumar, Hira, and Jogi stand closer to each other to some extent. The Tai Ahom stand apart. The situation is more or less the same in case of Deuri. The Mishing and Moran form another sub-cluster. The Chutiya and Maria seem to come closer.

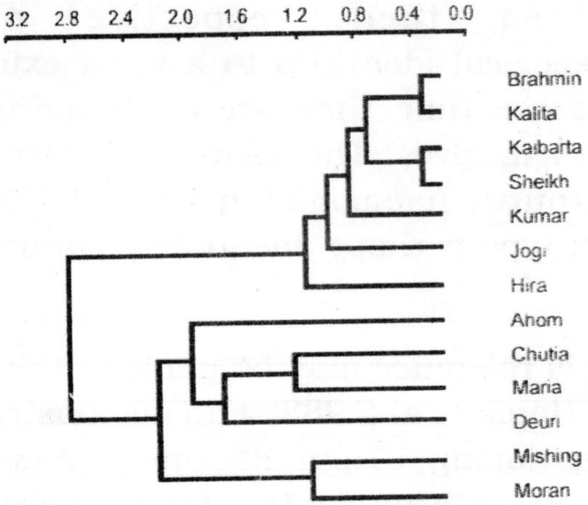

Fig. 3. Hiemaux distance ($\Delta g \times 10^{-3}$)-based on 13 quantitative traits and 8 qualitative traits including ABO blood groups and PTC taste sensitivity - among 13 populations of the Brahmaputra valley.

The foregoing discussion dealing with some of the factors involved in the ongoing processes resulting in populations variabilities illustrates two other processes, namely, fission and fusion, in which, however, also the basic factors for bringing genetic variations play their respective roles.

In comparison to whole of India, Assam is a

small geographic region where these processes are ongoing resulting in populations variation, forming different human populations groups, shaping various types out of the same original forms and so forth. Some of these processes are undoubtedly still continuing in other parts of India as well. If we perceive the situations in the perspective of whole of India, where ecological differences and socio-cultural variations are more, ethnic groups are of different origins, etc., then we will be able to gain an insight into what can happen in different parts of the country. That is why in chapter three mention about possibility of formation of different types of Mediterranean, Indo-Aryan, etc., was made.

Further, we have noted that microevolutionary dynamics can give rise to one type of populations from another. In this case, as has already been pointed out, time is a very important factor. One is to wait for a very long period to be able to detect the differences among the populationss involved. Evolutionary changes always proceed at a very lower rate. We referred to the possibility of evolution of the Dravidians from the Australoids. Sarkar (1962) wrote : "The present day inhabitants of South India, who cannot strictly be included within the Australoid ethnic strain, are such ecological variants. This combined with hybridization with the Indo-Aryan racial stock has led to a host of new combinations of physical features." In Anthropology human groups are studied in time and space perspective, taking into consideration all the processes which can have effect on them.

It was mentioned that it is believed by various scholars that the skeletal materials collected from different regions of the Indus valley civilization provide evidence of inhabiting the area at that time by representatives of different racial types. But the modern approaches to populations genetics have encouraged some scholars to reexamine the whole matter and to explain the variabilities among the populations due to microevolutionary dynamics and so forth instead of affiliating them to different racial groups.

According to a hypothesis put forwarded by Flatz in 1967 there is a positive correlation between haemoglobin E and Austroasiatic language speakers. This haemoglobin variant emerged in an Austroasiatic people and subsequently diffused throughout southeast Asia and then to other places. To test this hypothesis in 1972 Flatz and his colleagues examined the Khasi and Ahom for this gene, among whom they found high prevalence of HbβE, and thus the hypothesis was supported. On that basis it was suggested by them about the migration and spread of Austroasiatic tribes to Assam in prehistoric times to which references has already been made. At that time this observation was plausible. But subsequent studies (Das *et al* 1975, 1980) revealed that the frequency of this gene is still higher among some. Tibeto-Burman tribes, like the Kachari, Garo, Rabha, Tiwa. Therefore, it has become necessary to rethink and reexamine the whole matter before excepting any view. Perhaps the gene originated independently in two places among two different populationss (Deka *et al* 1988). The purpose of mentioning this event is to make one conscious of the fact that addition of new information may lead to development of new ideas.

ENDING

Finally, keeping in view all the above information, we can identify certain major factors as regards the peopling of Assam. Broadly speaking the first factor can be designated by the letters, *MM* which stands for Mythical Migration of people at very early time. The second factor is *FP*, that is, they were distributed over different areas laying the Foundation of the People. The third one is *AM* : Ancient Migration of different people at different times from different directions having different ethnic affiliations. The fourth factor may be called *PF*, which stands for Populations Formation by several factors, for example, tribal/populations identity, caste/tribe endogamy, religion, language. etc. The fifth factor,

OP includes all the Ongoing Processes affecting the biology of the populations, for example, gene flow, genetic drift, selection, etc. The last factor can be called *ER*, and that is, the End Results—an admixtured people of Assam.

Bibliography

Ali, A.N.M. Irshad : *Social Relations among the Assamese Muslims in Rural and Urban Situation.* Unpublished Ph. D. Thesis, Gauhati University, Guwahati, 1974.

— : Hindu-Muslim Relations in Assam. *Man in India,* 59, 4, 1979.

— : Influence of Indigenous Folk Traditions on the Assamese Muslims. *Assam Academy Review,* 1985.

Barua, B.K. : *A Cultural History of Assam (Early Period),* Vol.I. Nowgong, 1951.

Barua, K.L. : Alpines in Eastern India. *IC,* III, L., 1936.

Basu, R.N. : Blood groups among the Khasi. *Nature,* 142, 1938.

Bowles, G.T. : Linguistic and racial aspect of the Munda problem. *Mem. Peabody Museum Pap. An. Arch. Eth.,* XX, 1943.

Brown, J.C. and S.W. Kemp : Abors and Galongs by Dunbar, *Mem. As. Soc. Beng*, Part V, 1915.

British Research Association : Blood groups among primitive people. *Nature*. 144, 1939.

Buchi, E.C. : *Anthropologie Tibetaine,* Paris, 1965.

Buxton, L.H.D. : *The People of Asia*. London, 1925.

Chatterjee, S.K. : Kirata-Jana-Krti : The Indo-Mongoloids.
— *Jr. As. Soc. Beng*. 1951.

Cappieri, M. : The population of the Indus Civilization. *Occ. Pap. Field Res. Proj.*, 1970.

— : Die Asialiaschen Proto-Mediterranean Ethno-Archol. Zeit. *Jahrgang,* 2, 1961.

Chatterjee, B.K. and G.D. Kumar : Racial elements in Proto-Harappan skeletal remains at Lathol. *Anthropology,* 1963.

Chaudhury, P.C. : *The History of Civilization of the Peoples of Assam*. Guwahati, 1966.

Chaudhury, T.K. : *Demographic Trends in Assam*. Delhi, 1982.

Chakravarty, S. K.: *Microevolutionary dynamics in a hybrid population, the Man of Meghalaya.* Unpublished Ph.D. Thesis, Gauhati University,

Guwahati, 1982.

Das., T.C. : *The Purum,* Calcutta, 1945.

Das, Farida Ahmed : *A Study on the genetic composition of the Assamese Muslims of Dibrugarh (Assam).* Unpublished Ph. D. Thesis, Dibrugarh University, 1977.

Das, B.M. : *Ethnic Affinitiesof the Rabha,* Guwahati, 1960.

— : *Variation in physical characteristics of the Khasi Population of North East India,* Guwahati, 1978.

— : *Microevolution.* Delhi, 1981.

— : *Anthropometry of the Tribal groups of Assam, India.* Miami, 1970.

— : Ethnic elements in Northeast India. *Rivista di Anthropologia,* LXII, 1982-83.

— : Somatic variability among some populations of South Goalpara, Assam *Proc. Nat. Ins. Sc.,* 30, 5 & 6, 1964.

— : Inheritance of cerumen type and its importance in populaton studies. *Man in India,* 57, 4, 1977

— : Cerumen types in some populations of Northeast India. *Anthropologist,* XXII, 1 & 2, 1975.

— : On some aspects of variation and ongoing human evolution, Presidential address, Section of Anth. & Arch. 66th Ind. Sc. Cong. Assoc. Hyderabad, *Man in India,* 59, 1, 1979.

— : Somatic variations among the Hills and Plains Garos of Assam. *Man in India,* 49, 2, 1960.

— : Somatic variability in South Goalpara, Assam; *Acta Genet. Med. Gemmel., 16, 2, 1967.*

— : Caste and head hair. *Indian Anthropologist,* 3, 1973.

— : Physical variation in three Assamese castes. *Anthrop. Anz.* 37, 3, 1979.

Das, B.M. R. Deka : Population study in Assam : ABO blood groups haemoglobin E and G-6-PD deficiency. *Anthrop. Anz.,* 43, 1, 1985.

— : Haemoglobin E in North-East India : A Review. *Ind. J. Phys. Anthrop. & Hum. Genet.,* 6, 1, 1980.

Das, B.M. and R. Deka and Renuka Das : ABO blood groups and Rh-factor in six populations of Assam. *Bull. Anth. Surv. Ind.* XXIX, 1 & 2, 1980.

Das, B.M. Ranjan Deka and Renuka Das : Haemoglobin E in six populations of Assam. *J. Indian Anthrop. Soc.,* 15, 1980

Das, B.M. Ranjan Deka and G. Flatz : Predominance of the haemoglobin E gene in a

Mongoloid population of Assam (India). *Human Heredity,* 30, 1975.

Das, B.M. and Irshad Ali : *Assamese (Muslim) in Muslim People : A World Ethnographic Survey.* ed. R.V. Weeks, U.S.A., 1974.

Das, B.M. Priya Bala Das, Renuka Das, H. Walter and Heidi Danker-Hopfe : Anthropological Studies in Assam, India.

2. Observations on Muslims, *Anthrop. Anz.,* Jg. 43, 4, 1985.

3. Observations on three Brahmin groups, *Anthrop. Anz,* Jg. 44, 1, 1986.

4. Observations on the Kalitas. *Anthrop. An., Jg. 44, 2, 1986.*

5. Observations on four further caste groups (Jogis, Hiras, Kumars, Kaibartas) *Anthrop. Anz.* Jg. 44, 2, 1986.

Das, B.M., P.B. Das, and R. Das : *Variation in physical characteristics in the Kaibartas of Assam.* Study No. 5, UGC sponsored scheme, Anth. Deptt. Gauhati University, 1980.

— : *A comparative study of physical anthropology of four Assamese castes — Jogi, Hira, Kumar and Kaibarta.* Study No. 7, UGC, sponsored scheme. Anth. Deptt. Gauhati University, 1980.

Das, B.M. and P.B. Das : Distance santhropometriques entre quarter castes de L' Assam, Ide. *L' Anthropologie* 77, 5-6, 1973.

Das. B.M., M.R. Chakravartti, H. Delbruck and G. Flatsz.: High prevalence of Haemoglobin E in two populations of Assam.
Humangenetik, 12, 264-266, 1971.

Daka, R, A.P. Reddy, B.N. Mukherjee, B.M. Das, S. Banerjee, M. Roy; B. Dey, K.C, Malhotra and H. Walter :
Haemoglobin E distribution in Ten Endogamous population groups of Assam, India, *Hum Hered*, 38, 261-266, 1988.

Danker-Hopfe, H, B.M. Das, H. Walter, P.B. Das and Renuka Das : Anthropological studies in Assam, India.
6 Differentiation process among Assamese populatons :
Anthrop, Anz. 46, 2, 159-184, 1988.

Das. B.M., M.R. Chakravartti, H. Delbruck and G. Flatsz.: High prevalence of HGaemoglobin E in two populations of Assam.

Humangenetik, 12, 264-266, 1971.

The Brahmaputra Valley Population, Allahabad, 1997.

Eickstedt, E. Frh. V. : *Rassenkunde and*

Rassengeschichte der Menschheit. Stuttgart, 1934.

Endle, S. : *The Kacharis,* 1911.

Haemoglobin E and Beta-thalassaemia: their distribution in Thailand. Ann Hum Genet, 29, 151-170, 1965.

Dutta, B. : Anthropological Notes on some Assam castes. *Anth. Paper.* 5, Calcutta University, 1931.

Dixon, R.B. : The Khasis and the racial history of Assam. *Man in India,* 2, 1922.

Flatz, G. : Haemoglobin E : distribution and population dynamics. *Humangenetik,* 3, 1967.

Flatz, G., M.R. Chakravarti, B.M. Das and H. Delbruck. Genetic survey in the populations of Assam. 1. ABO blood groups, glucose-6-phosphate dehydrogenase and haemoglobin type, *Human Heredity* 22, 1972.

Gait, E.A. *History of Assam* : Third revised edition, 1963.

Guha, B.S. and P.C. Basu : A report on the human relics recovered by the Naga Hills (Burma) Expedition for abolition of human sacrifices during 1926-27. *Anth. Bull. No. I, Zoo, Surv. Ind.,* 1931.

Giudrida-Ruggeri, V. : *The first outlines of a systematic anthropology of Asia.* Calcutta, 1921.

Hutton. J.H. : *The Angami Nagas,* London, 1921.

Hutton, J.H. : *Census of India*, Vol. I, Part I, 1931.

Haddon, A.C. : *The Races of Man.*, Cambridge, 1924.

Iyer, L.A.K. : The racial history of South India, *Ind. Sc. Cong. Assoc.*, 1936.

Keane, A.H. : *Man—Past and Present,* 1920.

Keith, A : Review of B.S. Guha's Racial Affinities of the People of India. *Man,* 29, 1936.

Macfarlane, E.W.E. : Tibetan and Bhotia blood groups distribution. *Jr. As. Soc. Beng.*, 7, 1941.

Mitra, P.N. : Blood groups of the Angami Nagas of Assam. *Ind. Jr. Med. Res.*, 63, 1936.

Mill, J.P. : The Mros of Chittagong Hills. *Census of India,* Vol. 1, Part III, Appendix B, 1935.

Majumdar, D.N. : *Races and Cultures of India,* Bombay, 1965.

Olivier, G. : Physical anthropology of the Nagas of Assam. *Man in India,* 38, 2, 1958.

Oliver, D.L. and W.W. Howells : Microevolution : Cultural elements in physical variation. *Amer. Anth.*, 59, 6, 1957.

Phookan, M.N. : *Intratribal relations of the Kacharis in respect of anthropometry, ABO blood groups and taste sensitivity to PTC,* Unpublished

Ph. D. Thesis, Dib. Univ., Dibrugarh, 1974.

Playfair, A . : *The Garos, 1909.*

Risley, H. : *The People of India.* Calcutta, 1915.

Raichoudhury, T.C. : The Khasis, *Jr. Dept. Lett.*, Calcutta University, XXVI, 1935.

Sankalia, H.D. T.C. Sharma The Prehistoric Age. In *The Comprehensive History of Assam* Vol. I Ed. H.K Barpujari, Guwahati, 1990.

Sarkar, S.S. : Race and Race movement in India, *Cultural Heritage of India,* Calcutta, 1958.

— : Races and Cultures of India, *Rupam,* Inaugural issue, 1962.

— : *Ancient Races of Baluchistan, Panjab and Sind.* Calcutta, 1964.

— : *The Aboriginal Races of India.* Calcutta, 1954.

Sarkar, S.S. and P. Bhattacharjee : The Tribal Population of West Bengal. *Man in India, 38, 1, 1958.*

Sarkar S.S. *et al.* : A Physical Survey of the Kadar of Kerala. *Deptt. Anth. Govt. Ind. Memoir* 6, 1959.

Sharma, T.C. Northeast India in Prehistoric Times. In *The Tribes of Northeast India* Ed. S. Karotemprel, Calcutta 1-12, 1984.

Singh, K.S. : *Bio-anthropological Study of Three Populations in Manipur Valley.* Unpublished Ph.D. Thesis, Poona University, 1978.

Singh. S. : A contribution to Angami and Sema somatology. *Jr. As. Soc., Beng.,* 1935.

Shaw, W. : Notes on the Thado Kukis, *Jr. As. Soc. Beng.,* XXIV, 1928.

Sewell, R.B.S. and B.S. Guha : Report on the human remains excavated at Mohenjodaro. *Indus Valley Civilization* edited by J. Marshall, II, 1931.

Suri, R. : *Physical anthropology of the Angami Naga, a tribe of Northeast India,* Unpublished Ph.D. Thesis, Gauhati University, Guwahati, 1986.

Waddell, L.A. : The Tribes of the Brahmaputra Valley, *Jr. As. Soc. Beng.,* 69, 3, 1901.

Index